A BIRD IN MY BED

A daily stroll around our compound in Arizona

A Bird in My Bed

Anne Dunbar Graham
Fellow of the Royal Society of Arts
Illustrations by the author

FOREWORD
by
BRIAN VESEY-FITZGERALD

PELHAM BOOKS

First published in Great Britain by
PELHAM BOOKS LTD
52 Bedford Square
*London, W.C.*1
1971

© 1971 *by Anne Dunbar Graham*

7207 0473 1

Set and printed in Great Britain by
Tonbridge Printers Ltd, Peach Hall Works, Tonbridge, Kent
in Plantin ten on twelve point on paper supplied by
P. F. Bingham Ltd, and bound by James Burn
at Esher, Surrey

Contents

Illustrations

Author and publisher wish to thank the following for permission
to use the photographs as here indicated: No. 6, The Cunard
Steamship Co. and Stewart Bale & Co., Liverpool; No. 9, George
Ballantine Ltd and Fitzgerald-Owens Agency; Nos. 12 and 13,
The Zoological Society of London.

Acknowledgements

My sincere thanks and grateful appreciation of their efforts on behalf of Solomon and Sheba, as well as myself and this book, are particularly due to Mr Peter Olney, B.Sc., Dip.Ed., F.L.S. – Curator of Birds at London Zoo; Mr J. J. Yealland, F.L.S. (the former Curator) and indeed to the entire staff of the Parrot House at London Zoo who have all been exceptionally kind and helpful. To my mother who lavished a great deal of care and attention on both birds. To Mrs Joyce Wilkins, B.A., who gave so much of her time and valued advice in editing this work. To Mr J. W. Hardy, the eminent American ornithologist, Mr Colin Platt, veterinary field officer for I.S.P.A., the staff at Kew Gardens and the Natural History museum. Last, but by no means least, to all my relatives and friends, throughout the world, and whether or not actually mentioned in this story, whose interest in its progress has been such an encouragement.

Ode to Solomon

Solomon, Solomon, green as a pea,
With his crest of flame, is as gay as can be,
For he loves to swing in our old orange tree!

Here he screeches and whistles at all passers-by,
But sometimes gets frightened, when to Anne he'll fly,
To have his head stroked, and becomes coy and shy!

He feasts on nuts, on honey from bees,
On grapes, apples, carrots and sometimes on cheese,
With cream on the table, he starts to say please!

From Mexico comes this parrot of ours,
And he loves to bathe, in warm rain showers,
Yet, loudly he'll welcome the sunshine hours!

His cage a white castle, with branches entwined,
Is where he retires, soon after he's dined
On seeds of the sunflower, to dream of his kind!

Our dear little Solomon's no longer free,
But still I hope, he's gay as can be,
For now by his side snuggles Sheba, his bride!

Foreword

By Brian Vesey-FitzGerald

This is the story of Solomon, a Petz's Conure. In the United States he would be known as a 'Half-Moon Parrot' and in the United Kingdom as an Orange-fronted Conure. I hope that you will agree with me that his proper name is much to be preferred to either.

The conures are central and south American parrakeets. There are a number of species, the smallest being about the size of a budgerigar and the largest measuring 17 inches, which is smaller than the Amazon parrots. The Petz's Conure is a medium-sized member of the group. In shape conures are somewhat like macaws and in temperament they are nothing like budgerigars (which are also parrakeets), but very much like parrots. And that is really important. For there are very few books about parrots and certainly not one like this. So this fills a gap.

I have never owned a conure. But I have lived with a Blue-fronted Amazon parrot, which came to me late in life and with a taste for gin and a dislike of men. Mutual trust was achieved (painfully and bloodily on my part) and it was a sad day when she died, suddenly and without any notification of illness. Now I live with an African Grey with a taste for sherry and hymns, intelligent conversation and exotic oaths. I am a devotee of parrots. I think that a parrot makes a better pet than a dog or a cat (though, of course, the ideal is to have all three) and is very much less trouble than either. I may never have owned a conure. But I know that Miss Graham knows and understands parrots. She knows, for example, that no parrot should ever be kept *in* a cage; but should have the door open and be free to come and go at will. This is something too many parrot-owners do not fully appreciate, being afraid that the bird will escape. Parrots are home-lovers. Those few that do escape, escape from prison. And I know that Miss Graham's deep understanding springs from personal, and sometimes painful, experience. I know, because I have been down the same road. Though every parrot – and every conure: consider Solomon and Sheba – is an individual and determined to be as different as possible from every other parrot, all start with the same view of humans. So we all tread the same road to begin with.

This is a delightful book. Miss Graham is a born storyteller and very, very good company. You can read her book for sheer pleasure; as a first-rate travel book, as a chapter of autobiography, and never mind about parrots. But the really delightful thing about all this is that, if you do, it is odds-on you will end up with a parrot.

Brian Vesey-FitzGerald

Chapter I
Mexican Meeting

The roads were rough, hot, dusty and crowded with sheep, goats and donkeys, whose panniers bulged with vegetables, being led by small, bright-eyed chattering boys. Farmers, craftsmen and merchants were also laden with comestibles, such as live cockerels strung together by their legs. No one it seemed minded being so burdened since all were off to market at El Canaria where, after exchanging produce and catching up on local news, they would enjoy themselves at a Bull or Cockfight. Many of the crowd were singing, some to the sharp trill of a fipple flute, played by a fat gaucho sitting atop his already laden donkey, while others hummed to various tunes, strummed by shepherds, on guitars; yet the total effect was one of surprising harmony.

A large white American car, its roof down, crept along in the midst of this merry throng. Everyone knew that although the car was 'americano' the senorita driving it was 'inglesa'. They knew this because the senorita (me) driving the car (mine) was talking to one of the bright-eyed little boys called Pedro, who was trying hard to sell me one of his many sombreros. Having started at $5, Pedro was soon asking $1, and knew very well that his victim was weakening! Suddenly he grinned broadly: '*Senorita inglesa,*' he gasped, through exaggerated panting, 'I have moucho good idea: I ride americano car, sombrero 50 cents. *Si?*' he queried, affecting a limp and trying hard to look dejected, but he couldn't for long keep the impish grin from his eyes or face. I started laughing and, with a shriek of joy, Pedro, taking this as a sign of approval for his scheme, jumped into the back seat, before leaping over to join me in the front.

'*Senorita inglesa* make moucho hard bargain,' said he, plonking an enormous sombrero on my head to seal our deal as he bounced gleefully upon the well-sprung upholstery; for although the car was going no faster than the surrounding pedestrian crowd, Pedro, thrilled by his ride, was quite unable to keep still. He waved and shouted excitedly to his friends, until presently he asked cajolingly: 'Maybe Senorita you like my amigos ride your car too?' continuing: 'I get 1 peso each, Senorita. For this I show you round El Canaria,' adding with emphasis: 'Cost you nothing!'

Pedro was such an appealing little rogue I was powerless to resist, so before I could wink an eye the car was full to overflowing. Twelve or more people, a lamb, a string of cockerels, to say nothing of bundles of produce, were squashed inside. Others made full use of the expansive boot and yet more perched on the equally expansive bonnet. To this latter encroachment I did object, protesting that I could no longer see the way ahead; this, however, was not considered an obstacle by the merry masses thereon. Ridiculous promises of 'We will guide you Senorita,' came from all concerned, hastily accompanied by a shower of pesos for Pedro! I gave up and had a hilarious, if wearing, two hours that were full of song, as guide they did, right into the centre of El Canaria. It says much for the solidity of my trusty Oldsmobile that it bore this fearsome load without so much as a creak of protest.

About three miles before reaching El Canaria the road plunged through a forest, deliciously cool after the hot bright sun, yet it was by no means peaceful there. Noisy monkeys swung nimbly through the trees. Swooping past them, with penetrating screeches, were beautiful green parrots. All of this excited the domestic animals, who joined in by braying, baaing, bleating and crowing, as loud as they could; so much so that the human's gibble-gabble became almost inaudible.

On arrival at the market square, my Oldsmobile lost its loquacious passengers as fast as they had come, but not before they had given their '*amiga inglesa*' warm thanks, accompanied by hearty thumps on my back, or the bonnet of the car! I watched them for a time, whilst getting my breath back, bemused a little by the hot sun and noise, which somehow had intensified since we left the forest. It was the quiet but restless tone of 'Come Senorita' which made me aware that, true to his word, Pedro had stayed to show me around El Canaria.

The market was of course the centre of activity that day and I saw little else of the township. Savoury smells of hot tacos, tortillas, roasting corn and other food filled the air. People laughed and teased good humouredly as they jostled each other around, buying, selling or bartering their jewellery, fruit, pottery, halters, the local liquor and many things besides. The 'stalls' generally consisted of cloths spread on the ground, where merchants sat proudly amidst their wares. Other vendors, like Pedro, who incidentally managed to sell three more sombreros within half an hour, moved around.

Eventually I spotted a tiny bamboo cage, filled with a dozen or more beautiful small parrots, like those I had noticed in the forest. Pedro, quick to notice my distress on seeing them in miserable captivity, for once appeared at a loss for words. He was clearly puzzled that I thought this treatment cruel. 'Just birds,' he shrugged: 'What else you do with them?' 'Well,' I exclaimed, 'I would like to buy every single one and set them all free again, to live as they should, in the forest.' It was a rash statement because although Pedro gaped at me in disbelief for a moment; he saw in these remarks a chance to indulge in some more bargaining.

In a flash he was haggling with the trader – on my behalf! There was no holding him, but since the merchant was asking $68 for each parrot – buying one, let alone all, seemed quite out of the question as I had just a little over $40 left. Eventually I managed to impress Pedro with this sad fact, but it merely encouraged him to go on. He was not to be outdone! More rapid exchanges in Spanish followed until finally Pedro turned to me beaming, having secured, as he stressed, a bargain. 'Maybe four, maybe six months,' said he excitedly. Not without qualms I handed over the $38 asked for, but the recent impression of beautiful creatures flying free contrasted so sharply with the glazed eyes and huddled misery of those in the cage, I decided that it was after all but a small price to pay, to return even one to freedom.

My musing was rudely interrupted: 'Senorita like?' The grinning merchant held out a parrot for inspection. He did not wait for a reply but, with ghoulish delight, or so it seemed, popped the bird unceremoniously into a greasy brown paper bag that had until recently held his lunch of cheese tacos, and still smelled strongly of them. My protest was halted by the merchant's next utterance: 'You let go – Periquito no live; him too young, Senorita, him have moucho bad wing – him no fly.' He grinned widely as he said this, showing his tobacco-stained, broken teeth. An A.D.C. to Mephistopheles I thought to myself, worried that I was lumbered with a parrot I could not let go, and knew far too little about to keep. Yet my sentiments towards all animals, particularly those in distress, precluded me from persuading the merchant to take the pathetic creature back.

I tried to talk soothingly to the parrot on the way back to my 'Olds', but there was neither sound nor movement from the bag. I opened it and peeped in – a baleful eye, surrounded by crinkled yellow flesh, met mine and blinked. I left the bag partially opened for air and proceeded with all possible haste towards the border. Speed, however, made for a bumpy ride over the rough roads, in spite of super springing and individual wheel suspension. The poor little bird must have been extremely frightened and I wondered if it was in pain, for I had noticed on close inspection that the badly damaged wing was due to an extremely bad job of wing-clipping. Blood had coagulated with dirt upon it, but there was little I could do for the parrot's comfort at that time.

It seemed an unending journey to the 'twin' border towns of Tijuana, but eventually we arrived and were safely through Customs on both sides. The American officer was particularly easy-going and courteous. He made the usual check for plants or fruit, and seeing only an Ali Baba type pottery vase on the back seat, gave me a quick all-clear. Then, as I had decided to have the roof up (the next half of the trip being a breezy freeway) the officer offered his help in clipping it down. Subsequently I remembered the parrot and asked if he could tell me where the nearest pet shop was located.

'San Diego, ma'am.' The town being eighty miles on, his reply astonished me until he continued speaking, halting my tale of the parrot, which, as it turned out, was just as well, since – 'We don't go much for pet shops here, ma'am, they encourage parrot smuggling – as you very rightly guessed,' he went on. Thankfully I realised that he had only half-grasped my unfinished sentence, mis-hearing it through the whirring of the motor bringing the roof up. Having completely forgotten about importation regulations I was wondering whether or not to declare the parrot when the officer leant into the car, clipping its top in position. His eyes went to the taco bag, from which a strong smell of cheese still emanated.

'Great stuff those tacos,' he commented. Thinking of the possibly dreadful fate that could befall the little parrot should it move or screech, I reluctantly kept quiet, but suddenly felt sick with apprehension. 'Why, ma'am, you do look pale,' the officer's voice sounded concerned. 'Too many tacos maybe,' he jokingly continued, intimated that he would not mind any that remained.

'Just a doggy bag,' I fibbed in quick reply, grateful for this highly respectable, but peculiarly American institution of carrying left-overs around!

The officer seemed such a pleasant young man that I almost began to doubt he would be party to the diabolical cruelty, in which some American port and border authorities are reputed to indulge, when killing off any illegally imported animals. Thus, probing him on the matter, I asked if indeed they returned such creatures from whence they came. 'No ma'am, they're disposed of,' his answer came harshly. Obviously none of J. J. Audubon's humane ideals had rubbed off on to him.

Thus, although I had been an unwitting smuggler to start with, then a rather reluctant one, I was now firmly resolved to remain one! No animal in my care was going to be 'disposed of', particularly in these days of 'humane' killers, in the unnecessarily brutal manner I had been told about. My decision not to declare the parrot was really spurred by a recent report sent by a friend then working on a Chinese freighter. He had written that a few of the crew had purchased some parrots in Buenos Aires. On arrival at New Jersey, a port inspector had, on seeing the parrots, picked up a pair and bashed their heads together, finishing them off, with apparent vindictive glee, by swinging them against the cabin wall. Thus he killed the dozen or more that were on board. The ship's cat was then 'disposed of' in similar manner. I have omitted the gory details of this vile crime, the bare facts are sickening enough, although I have since been profoundly shocked hearing similar tales from an American cousin.

Actually these tales surprised me since following the Scandinavian countries, Americans, though noticeably unsentimental towards animals, have one of the best records for conservation with all their wildlife reserves given not only Federal but State aid. Their splendid results are delightfully evident in superb national parks like 'Yellowstone' where, I feel, the ideal has been achieved.

Needless to say I was more than a little relieved when I at last got under way again. Although at the border I had been grateful to providence for seeing to it that the little parrot had been given to me in a taco bag, I was worried at the many hours it had been there, so was dismayed to find San Diego's stores closed for the day – not really surprising since it was nearly 9 p.m. Then I remembered Farmers Market, in Hollywood, which stays open nearly all night, and that the hi-way to Los Angeles was fast-moving. Thankfully I found the market's pet shop open; $5.80 purchased a small brass cage, but adequate for the temporary measure that I hoped it would be. I spoke, as I thought, soothingly, to the parrot and slowly put my hand into the taco bag – it was swiftly withdrawn. I then knew that even small parrots have powerful beaks! Bud, the pet shop owner, was from experience wiser than I and, turning the cage on its side, he tipped the bag's contents into it. With a justifiably indignant shake of its feathers, the parrot clambered stiffly to the topmost perch, glowering at us with suspicion, its body quivering with fear. 'Poor little thing,' I said, sucking my bleeding finger, whilst pondering on what I was going to do with this pathetic, bedraggled creature, looking quite unlike his gorgeous compatriots in the forest.

If Bud wondered how I came to be in possession of the parrot he gave no indication of doing so, but plied me with sunflower seeds, millet sprays and a mirrored plastic bath. Knowing nothing of parrot habits or needs at that time, I asked for a guide book on the subject, but the market was bereft of any, as were libraries that I tried next day. Worse still was the complete dearth of vets, in the Los Angeles area, who knew anything at all about parrots. This was particularly disturbing as there was no equivalent of Britain's R.S.P.C.A. that one could call on for help or advice. Much later, on a second-hand bookstall, I was delighted to find an excellent comprehensive guide, *Parrots and Parrot-like Birds* by the 12th Duke of Bedford. Unfortunately this really interesting book is now out of print, and even second-hand copies are more or less impossible to come by.

Meanwhile, Bud told me that the bird was a 'Half Moon' parrot (more correctly called a Petz's Conure) and thought it had most likely been caught in the rain forests of Brazil. Beyond that he knew little since they have rarely been kept in captivity, and until recently no one seems to have made a study of them in the wild. Actually Bud's information was somewhat inaccurate (see Chapter 10), but in any event I left the pet shop very little wiser as to what procedures would be best for the parrot's welfare. 'The main thing,' Bud had said, 'is to keep it in a warm, draught-free place,' which was simple enough in the mild Californian climate. What did prove to be a problem was the intrusive Los Angeles smog.

The next two days were most disheartening, the 'Half Moon' trembling with fear every time someone went near him. He did not touch his seeds or water and uttered not one sound, nor did he make any attempt to come out of the cage, although its door was left open all day. My maid, who did not care much for birds, predicted with a certain morbid satisfaction, that the parrot was about to die. Certainly he looked as though he might. Feathers that were not clogged with dirt 'stared' and he sat hunched in abject misery. To make matters worse, I noticed his eyes becoming red and knew they must be sore and smarting from the insidious smog which invaded even the air-conditioned apartment.

Although I had shelled seeds for the conure, thinking that perhaps he was too young to do so himself (happily a wrong surmise), on the third morning, when I discovered that none had yet been eaten, I felt that the time had come for drastic action if the maid's morbid prediction was not to be fulfilled. Water seemed the first necessity, so having armed myself with a pair of leather gloves and found a clean plastic eye-dropper, I caught the parrot, not without difficulty. Holding him as gently as possible, I managed to force some drops of water into his beak. This was easier than I had expected since he had grabbed hold of the dropper and I was then able to stroke under his gullet, making him swallow. Meanwhile, since I had hold of him, I treated his eyes to an extra mild solution of boracic and warm water. I then put him back in the cage, to give us both a breather for he had fought strenuously during the above treatment; however I was determined that if he had not eaten of his own accord within the next few hours, I would force feed him with pellets of crushed seed.

Meanwhile I treated my wounds, for the parrot had managed to bite through the gloves and my wrists were badly scratched. On my return to the living-room he stretched out his neck and screeched at me in a most abusive manner. That at least was a good sign, but when I went near the cage he again cringed away, getting into a miserable huddle.

My work is in the field of interior design and mural painting, and when, later that morning, I had to go out to finish a job, I decided to take the conure with me. My client's house was situated in the hills above Los Angeles and as we motored up, its pall of smog was left behind. The air became fresh and we saw the sun for the first time since our return to the States. I had left the cage uncovered and chatted to the little conure in 'birdy' noises. By the time we arrived he was beginning to take a cautious interest. I left him by an open window in the dining-room, where he would be well away from the smell of paint. The sun streamed in on him and the chattering of garden birds could be heard, but as I was to be working in another room I shut the cage door and was pleasantly surprised when he tried to nip me through the bars, instead of cringing away.

Some three hours later my client, coming in to announce coffee and a light lunch, exclaimed: 'My, honey, you sure do have a hungry bird!' She was not exaggerating; on entering the dining-room I got a truly happy surprise. The conure was by then venting his spleen on the millet spray, scattering its seeds to the far corner of the room. Sunflower seeds and moistened oats had all been eaten, leaving a mound of shells and husks, also a quantity of water had been splashed around. It was a great relief to see the messy aftermath of the little parrot's meal. Fortunately, my client was extremely understanding and did not mind the shambles one bit. In fact, knowing the predicament I was in, due to my lack of ornithological knowledge, she had arranged that a friend of hers, an expert in the subject, should come over to my apartment the next day. Meanwhile, when I put a hand on the cage, the parrot attempted to attack it, between his destructive foray on the millet spray. His eyes were brighter and it was evident that his will to live was really back.

Many years previously I had been told that if an animal, such as a cat, is pining away for any reason, and a dog is encouraged to attack or chase it, the cat's adrenalin juices react automatically to preserve its life, making it either rush for cover, or turn to attack the enemy. Either way the pining spell is thereby broken, and so it starts living normally again. Thus I presume that the unintentional fright I had given the conure that morning in catching him and giving him water etc. had worked in the same way. It certainly seemed so from the way he had fought and later screeched at me.

Early next morning I was awakened by the happy sound of cracking seeds. The smog had cleared and the sun was shining so I lifted the cage on to the balcony. Abe Solomons, my client's friend, arrived sharp at 10 a.m. and was able to give me a great deal of welcome advice. Actually it was after him that I called the parrakeet 'Solomon' for, as we relaxed over coffee, which the maid had brought out to the balcony, he told me a delightful 'tall story' about his grandfather's parrot, a truly wise old bird who had brought him lots of money! Viz:—His grandfather, waiting at a pet shop to pick up his wife's poodle from its weekly beauty treatment, heard a parrot speaking Yiddish which tickled his fancy, so he bought the bird and they soon became firm friends. Singing was amongst the parrot's accomplishments which gave old Abe the idea of teaching it an appropriate psalm for Rosh Hoshanah. (Abe being out of favour with the local Rabbi at the time, thought to please him this way.) The day the festival dawned they set out early, and the parrot sitting proudly on Abe's shoulder was singing the psalm perfectly until, that is, they reached the synagogue where, on hearing the disbelieving bets of Abe's friends regarding its ability, the parrot sat haughtily dumb. Nevertheless old Abe, assuming he was on to a certainty, accepted and doubled many bets, until finally, as his parrot remained stubbornly silent, he realised he was broke!

His friends went off laughing and as Abe turned despondently homewards, his parrot started chuckling too. 'You daft old bird,' said grandfather Abe, 'You've ruined me,' but, on hearing the bird's answer, he too began to smile, since his wise and feathered pal had said: 'My dear old friend, you're forgetting Yom Kippur in nine days' time. Just think what odds we'll get then!' 'And that,' the grandson concluded, 'was how the family started its fortune!'

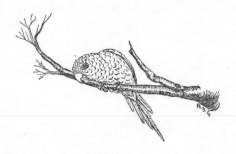

I christened Solomon that very afternoon by giving him a shower. The sun was blazing hot, so I then cooled myself off in the pool. I had taken the cage down with me and Solomon seemed very interested in my aquatics. He began to make answering noises when I talked to him and for the first time I noticed him taking an interest in his appearance, thoroughly preening his feathers, so that by the time he was dry they looked almost iridescent in the sunlight and lapped smoothly over his body. Having done this he began rubbing his head, in a thoroughly soppy way, against a twiggy perch that I'd installed in his cage.

I kept Solomon with me as much as possible, but although he made noises of recognition and answered back (in parrot language) whenever I spoke to him, he was still afraid of my hand, which, on the advice of Abe Solomons, I held frequently in the cage. Gradually the conure accepted its presence without becoming panic-stricken, but still retreated, although it was always offered full of seeds.

Some three weeks after I got Solomon I took him with me on a trip to Santa Barbara. This time, with cage door shut, I left the car hood down. Balmy air pleasantly mitigated the scorching sun on the winding coast road. Solomon seemed to enjoy the ride, screeching excitedly as for the first time he made an effort to flap his wings, sadly difficult in that small cage. Later he attempted a bath, also unsuccessful as the container tipped over flooding out both cage and front seat. Undeterred he preened elaborately, then dined 'Al Fresco', making a great 'do' of clambering awkwardly with one seed to the topmost perch where, with great dexterity, he would shell and dehusk it before eating delicately. He clung to the perch with one foot as he held the seed in his other 'paw', taking small bites and obviously savouring each one. Meanwhile he kept perfect balance as the car snaked round the many hairpin bends.

The working day was long, so darkness had fallen before we began the journey back. Solomon slept soundly most of the way, his head stretched right back, cradled under a wing, while he held the perch firmly with one foot, the other being tucked up tight against his breast. Once more I noticed that the car's movement had no detrimental effect on his balance. I stroked the top of his head very gently but he didn't stir until we drove into the brightly lit underground garage at our apartment block.

When we got in Solomon began digging vigorously round his seed dish until it became obvious that none was left. He demanded a refill by banging sharply on the container with his beak. Late as it was, I persevered with offering him the seeds in my hand. For a few moments he sat quite still, looking curiously at me. Then cautiously he put his head down a little, eyeing me and the seeds for another longish pause. Suddenly, with a quick dart, he had taken a seed, retreated to the perch furthest from my hand, and begun to eat. This momentous step forward in our relationship was soon to be followed by an even bigger one. I had managed to keep my hand quite still and after Solomon had taken a few seeds in this way, his confidence grew until he stepped down from his perch on to the pad of my thumb, where he ate slowly, still keeping a wary eye upon me. When he had finished he took hold of my thumb with his beak and gently squeezed it, before hopping back on to his perch.

I withdrew my hand slowly, then filled his seed cups. Solomon had begun rocking sleepily but when I made some 'Goodnight' noises (similar to 'Radio Kisses'), he answered in perfect imitation and although my hand still rested on the cage, he tucked his head back under his wing once more and went off to sleep. Solomon had, at last, begun to trust and perhaps accept me as a friend and the wonder of these moments is no doubt better imagined than described.

Chapter 2

A Fountain Bath

Although his cage door was always left open, Solomon never made any attempt to come out of it, which is one thing that puzzles me about his early behaviour. Thus by the weekend following our trip to Santa Barbara, nearly four weeks after my eventful Mexican visit, I felt it was high time that Solomon left his cage for a while at least, and I set about persuading him to do so.

Having tempted him on to my hand with seeds, I began slowly withdrawing it, but at the first slight movement he hopped quickly back to a perch, screeching abusively. He was not to be enticed again, so I passed my hand freely in and out of the ever open door to give him the idea of using it as an exit, and then removed the seed dish, leaving it within view. Solomon appeared to be not the slightest bit interested, and having glanced at my efforts with his head on one side, turned his back and looked bored. He had, however, 'got the message' and was only waiting for me to turn my back, which I did soon after, intending to get coffee. On reaching the kitchen area, I heard Solomon give a somewhat startled squawk as, at long last, he hopped out of the cage and began a slithery scrabble about the table.

Now that the little conure was out, I began to see just how bad a condition he was in. Apparently the weight difference caused by the cruel and unnecessary hacking of one wing was considerable and upset his balance, for he kept toppling over to that side. As was perhaps to be expected, he very soon fell from the table but, rejecting aid, scuttled off as best he could in his crippled condition to 'sanctuary', provided by a long low coffee table. There he rested, the foregoing effort having made him pant in an almost convulsive manner, but as he still clearly wanted no helping hand from me, I sat back to enjoy my coffee, while watching his exploration of the apartment, laboured as it was.

Solomon next clambered up the large sectional sofa, upholstered in a knobby-textured, white fabric, which provided an excellent – dare I say 'ideal'? – surface for a young parrot's climbing exercises. His approval of this particular stomping ground was obvious. Several times he clambered awkwardly up the back cushions, then hopped down upon the seat again, as if having a game, meanwhile making a great deal of what sounded like happy noises. Thus any slight dismay I felt that Solomon had chosen this most costly piece of upholstery upon which to limber up was mitigated by my pleasure at seeing him out and was dispelled all together when, after a time, he had the courtesy to leave, before depositing, with great aplomb, his calling card upon the coffee table which, being glass, was easily cleaned up. After such a display of consideration how could I have grumbled that the appearance of the sofa's area where he sat preening on his return, began to remind me of Candy Floss? – this since he chose to tease out the knobbles of fabric within his immediate vicinity.

Having completed his 'toilet' Solomon then began testing the full strength of his wings, his dark grey scaly legs straddled wide for balance. Nevertheless his movements to effect this were heartbreaking to observe, being jerky and pathetically uncertain. To my mind 'pinioning' (wing-clipping) is a barbaric practice that deserves heavy fines and prosecution, as does chaining, or for that matter, permanent caging. After all, even human prisoners, deservedly behind bars for despicable crimes, are permitted their daily hours of exercise.

Regrettable is hardly the word for the actions of a 'civilised', 'animal-loving' society, that had sense enough to abolish the 'Ball and Chain' for its criminal class centuries ago, but still permits such forms of medieval torture to be inflicted upon its defenceless, innocent creatures. It is not only incredible, it is unforgiveable, particularly when such atrocities are committed by so-called 'Sanctuaries' and zoos. How I agree with all that Konrad Z. Lorenz, of Germany, has had to say regarding 'pinioning', etc. Like him, I feel strongly that these offences should be punishable by law, and find it strange that in spite of the R.S.P.C.A.'s many invaluable works for animal welfare, they do not expand the scope of their activities to include campaigns that would effect this.

I should also like to see some law passed that would abolish the manufacture and use of the pitifully pokey cages made for the domestic pet market, thus assuring adequate, if minimal standards, for the physical and mental well-being of the all too often 'condemned' occupants of these contraptions. A healthy bird of any species is naturally very active, but cage it unsuitably for any length of time and it begins to suffer from ennui. One symptom of this fearful malaise is that they eventually show an unnatural reluctance to come out, or stay out, for long. To me it is terrible to see the bewilderment of a bird or animal so affected. Yet, incredible as it seems, some 'doting' owners mistake this malady for attachment, on the part of their pets, to their prisons.

As to Solomon and his new-found freedom, he eventually made his way to the bedroom, where he disappeared under the divan. My efforts to cajole him out were unsuccessful, even when I tried a bribe of seeds, although by then he had been awandering for over three hours and must have been getting hungry. It seemed that with his liberation his trust in me had diminished. Not wishing to force the pace, I placed the seeds at the foot of the bed and left him, briefly, to his own devices.

Shortly afterwards Abe Solomons arrived with his daughter and son-in-law. He had come with the idea of buying them a painting, but after they had been there an hour, they had happily purchased most of my furniture and accessories. This was the second time in three months that I had sold the apartment's appointments, but since I had the place decorated as a showroom for my specialised and exclusive lacquer techniques, this constant change was only to be expected, and gave me a welcome opportunity to experiment with new ideas.

It was as well that our business was concluded when Solomon graced us with his presence, since from that moment on he became the focal point of our attention to the exclusion of all else. I had been asked out to lunch with the Solomons family and did not feel it wise to leave the young conure out on his own at that stage. Solomon did of course resist our various efforts to catch him, and in spite of being hampered by his gammy wing, he managed to scuttle around with amazing dexterity, so there followed an obstacle race that was ridiculous, four adults chasing a wounded bird, a chase that lasted the best part of half-an-hour and left all five of us exhausted.

It was, however, with very mixed feelings that I regarded Solomon's eventual recapture. It was awful to see him once again huddled up in the cage, although on this occasion it was due more to fatigue than misery. It seemed an effort for him to try and keep his eyes open. Still, when I attempted to stroke the top of his head sympathetically he summoned enough energy to bite. However he took little notice when I shut the cage door, since at the time he was concerned with quenching his thirst in that seemingly laborious way that parrots have. Following his lead we four humans then downed a long iced refresher before leaving him to have a quiet nap while we went off to lunch.

Later that same afternoon Abe put out a hand for Solomon who went obediently on to it and sat passively while I fed him seeds. Then when Abe moved his hand back towards the cage door, Solomon hopped back on, of his own accord. The fact that Abe had kept a glove on during this episode had quite a lot to do with Solomon's sudden amenability, for when I tried this same procedure only minutes later, but with a bare hand, I got a really nasty bad-tempered bite. Yet when, at Abe's suggestion, I put gloves on and tried again, Solomon stepped hesitantly on to my hand allowing me to bring him out.

I have never been able to work out the reasoning that lay behind this quirk, but I was indeed thankful to have discovered it, in those early days, because it never failed to work, even if on occasion his beak clipped through the thick leather with no trouble whatsoever! At any rate, when, on that first evening, having been on my hand for a few minutes, he hesitantly indicated a desire to return to his cage, I made no move to stop him. He propelled himself in and although it was barely 5.30 p.m. soon fell fast asleep, so his day's exploration must really have worn him out. Even when later, I turned on lights and gramophone, he did not stir.

On waking next morning I was happy to find Solomon sitting atop the cage preening and making a fair amount of noise. There he stayed for most of the day, going inside only to eat or drink. He spent a fairly inactive day showing, fortunately, no inclination to repeat his exploration of the apartment, but during the next two weeks the time Solomon spent outside the cage well exceeded the time he stayed inside it, which naturally I was very pleased to see.

It had become evident that I was to be the one to nurse the young conure back to full strength so that he could eventually rejoin his fellows, although my original intention had been to hand him over to someone better qualified to look after him. The brass cage was obviously far too small for a lengthy sojourn, which it now looked like being, so I was delighted when there arrived from Abe the magnificent gift of a large, decorative antique cage. From the moment this cage arrived Solomon, instinctively knowing it was for him, registered excitement and it was not long before he took possession. He watched with impatience as I entwined it with branches and installed feeding cups. Bowing up and down on top of the little cage, he began tentatively stretching his wings. Finally he took off, landed at my feet and allowed me to lift him to its top, where he soon began clambering round until he found its door. In his anxiety to enter he lost his footing, falling with a heavy thud to its floor. However he seemed undeterred by this and quickly began an exploratory climb around the inside.

I had installed an old shaving mirror behind the seed and drinking cups and the magnified side was towards Solomon. When he caught sight of himself he let out a shrill shriek of excitement before paying homage to himself. His eyes contracted and his crown feathers became raised, much as a cockscomb would have, while he clicked his fleshy, thick black tongue sharply against his beak. This went on for some five or ten minutes then, after drawing himself up to his full height, he emitted more excited cries before drinking in an exaggerated and elaborated fashion. This he followed by washing his head in the water cup, before trying out the bath. His ablutions over, he returned to the shaving mirror, which he tilted down, and settled himself upon it to dry off.

Solomon's aquatics, though amusing to watch, left a somewhat soggy and not an altogether pleasant aftermath which, much to the maid's annoyance, was by no means confined to the immediate vicinity of the cage – so much so that I was not only relieved, but rather surprised, when she again came to work the next day. Her dislike of the little conure was rivalled only by his dislike of her. Accordingly he flew into a rage whenever she went near, particularly if she dared to lay a hand on his new cage. Yet it seemed that they delighted in taunting each other whenever possible. Even I was not exempt from Solomon's passion for laying claim to his territory. Several times he attacked my hand quite viciously, although I was merely filling seed cups, etc. I found it disturbing that nothing but a gloved hand would bring him out of this new habitat, and even then that he would scuttle back in with all possible haste. It was, I felt, a backward step in the progress he'd shown until then. The necessary stimulation to encourage him out came from a most unexpected source.

Solomon enjoying a favourite perch – an old orange tree, in our Arizona compound

Solomon relishes a sesame cracker while perched on his own indoor "tree"

It's thirsty work driving across deserts and Solomon quenches his, before we enter the workshop

Solomon busy at his tatting

It was early one morning when the furniture removers duly came and went and the new pieces were installed. Amongst them was a dolphin fountain for the hall and because this used a new type of pump, I decided to keep it going for several hours to ensure there were no hitches when clients came to view. I suddenly noticed that Solomon seemed very agitated and at first I thought this due to the morning's upheaval. For the first time in weeks he stepped smartly on to my hand when I put it out to him, instead of giving me what had become a customary 'handshake'. He scrambled quickly up to my shoulder and stayed thereabouts while I attempted to get on with my various activities. This was however no easy matter for although I tried speaking soothingly to Solomon he remained perturbed, and in between pacing my shoulders, kept giving my cheeks and ears light pecks. He was still unsettled when some 15 minutes later I went to check on how the fountain was working.

Solomon went beserk when we entered the hall; firstly he pulled himself up to the top of my head where he did his best to take off, but got hopelessly entangled. Having been extracted from my hair he crashed into the planter, backing the dolphin fountain. There he tore frantically at the leaves, as he attempted an unsuccessful climb up, seeming terrified when their slender stems bowed under his weight. He gripped hard with his beak when I put out a hand to assist him, but on passing the fountain's rim he catapulted off, landing with a tremendous splash. Undeterred, he scrambled to the side and watched the spray intently for a few minutes, and then began to play happily amongst it until he was thoroughly soaked. Ever after this he always made for the fountain when he heard it turned on, hobbling hurriedly across the floor if I did not take him there immediately.

From then on Solomon gradually increased the time he spent outside the antique cage and to my delight, started to exercise his wings at regular intervals. Vanity had much to do with this, for he performed his P.T. clinging to the outside of the cage, but facing the shaving mirror. Chattering excitedly he admired himself; Slowly spreading each of his wings in turn, showing off the true beauty of their colours, then having flapped them vigorously he began tirelessly preening the odd feather into place, until all lay to his satisfaction.

Now that Solomon had grown a full new suit of feathers he

really did look beautiful and seemed very much aware of this improvement in his appearance, fluffing his plumage out proudly whenever one looked at him. Briefly, his back and wings are a shimmering jade, his cheeks and 'bib' being a brownish olive, while his trousers are a bright lime green. His head sports a cap of dusty French blue, and forming a crescent between this and his beak, are tiny feathers of bright orange, which probably gives rise to the name 'Half-Moon' being colloquially applied to this species in America, as against the Golden Crowned Conure being known as the 'Half-Moon' in Europe. Long tail feathers match Solomon's blue cap, as do the primary wing feathers which are prettily streaked with turquoise (see Chapter 10 for full scientific description).

When Solomon spread his wings I was delighted not only to observe their beauty, but to see the diminishing gap where one wing had been hacked. I was also pleased to note the increasing vigour with which he flapped them, after he tired of primping. The draught from these exercises was so strong that papers, even at the far end of the room, started to flutter about. At first this startled Solomon, but as his strength grew so did his confidence and he soon began playing paper-chase games. Pouncing upon the letters, etc. he would gleefully tear them to shreds. After salvaging a near disaster with a cheque, and as it seemed likely this fad would become a habit, I was careful not to leave anything of papery importance within striking distance of his effective wing 'fan'. However, it seemed a shame to spoil his fun entirely, so I supplied sheets torn from used notebooks. Not surprisingly, perhaps, our maid never shared my amusement at Solomon's comical antics with them!

It was not long before Solomon began to spend many hours on my shoulder, where he spent much of the time gently preening my hair. In fact, I am convinced he spent longer on this operation than on tidying his own feathers, but just occasionally, if he came across a tangle, he would lose patience and one sharp tug would painfully uproot the offending hairs. Fortunately this did not happen too often or it would not have been long before I rivalled Yul Brynner!

As soon as Solomon began coming readily to hand I started taking him out to the secluded garden of some Hungarian friends where he sat, content enough, in an old vine covering their carport. These friends had a four-year-old daughter, Suzy, who soon became a great buddy of Solomon, and the two spent many happy hours hours playing together in a rubber paddling pool, Suzy sitting in the middle, splashing Solomon, who paced precariously round the rim. Sometimes when Suzy ran off to pursue another interest Solomon, with wings spread wide, would skim across the pool and pull his sodden self up the far side, digging his beak deep into the rubber and making me fear a puncture was imminent. Fortunately this somehow never occurred.

One thing Suzy and Solomon did not see eye to eye about was a large rubber ball, Solomon jumping nervously every time Suzy bounced it exuberantly round the compound. Finally the inevitable happened; the ball got out of control, bounced towards Solomon, went over his back and splashed into the pool. Fright gave Solomon the impetus to take off in a short upward flight on to the vine, which he climbed with remarkable speed. Once at the top he did a series of fluttery hops along the drainpipe until he reached the corner of the building. There, after catching his breath, he shattered the afternoon's quiet letting the neighbourhood know, in no uncertain terms, just how greatly he had been upset.

Suzy too was distressed and in tears at the seeming tragedy of Solomon buzzing off. It took a great deal to convince her just how encouraged I was by his first upward flight. Short as it was, it strengthened the hope that he would eventually be able to live a normal life. By the time Suzy was calm, Solomon too had ceased his protest, although he remained agitated. There was no hesitation in his downward glide, when I put an arm up and bid him come. Once on my shoulder, however, he gave my cheek a few sharp nips before biffing it vigorously with his beak.

When the time came to leave, Solomon clung tightly on to my shoulder as I made a move to put him back in his small brass cage, that was now used for transporting him from place to place. Since he was so clearly against it that afternoon, I let him remain where he was. He sat on my shoulder as good as gold while we drove back to the apartment through the heavy rush-hour traffic of Los Angeles. He never stirred and the only sound he made, which appeared to be one of contentment, was an occasional rasping of tongue against his beak, so I repeated the experiment next day. Again Solomon was no trouble. He

seemed instinctively aware that driving required my full concentration and never once made any attempt to attract my
attention to himself, which he was by then accustomed to doing
while in the apartment, should he feel I had left him to his own
devices for too long. Nor did he attempt to remove my spec's,
which normally he hated me wearing, and on one occasion
had broken in his anxiety to get them off. Thus this became our
established mode of travel.

There were only two things that caused Solomon distress
while we were in the car: one was squealing tyres of passing
'tearaway' drivers, and the other was when we visited the drive-
in section of our bank. For some reason he always got into a tizz
when the cash drawer slid out towards the car. Panic had the
unpleasant effect of making him leave unusually large droppings at
indiscriminate spots. Of course he did this in the normal course
of events, but I was gradually getting him trained to leave my
shoulder for a selected spot before depositing same, or alternatively, waiting on his chosen perch until he had performed, before
coming to me. Actually, after about eight or nine months he was
completely 'house-trained' in this respect, and, as a rule after that
any 'mishaps' were generally deliberate! He would never leave
favourite perches, however, such as the top of a door, to return to
his cage, so we had to take due precaution and supply strips of
washable plastic to slip under them.

There is only one bird I have ever come across that was
completely 'house-trained' and that was an Indian Mynah, be-
longing to a vet's wife, which obligingly took off to the 'loo' whenever nature called. There he used the perch his mistress had
provided over the lavatory. Yet he too has been known to disgrace
himself deliberately over an unpopular visitor! And who says
birds don't think? This misconception is strangely common although all birds, whether wild or in captivity, clearly demonstrate
this ability, in adapting themselves to strange situations, and in the
procuring of food. An amusing instance of the latter occurred
while we lived in India. Our usually imperturbable Alsatian bitch,
Cora, was one day provoked by crows into losing her bone to
them. Cora had been gnawing this contentedly in the compound
when one of two crows, who had been watching her from a
nearby Jacaranda tree, flew down and began making provocative
darts towards her snout, accompanied by raucous screeching.

Eventually our Alsatian took the challenge and leapt towards it. At this point the second crow swooped down, made off with the bone and was soon rejoined by its mate in the tree. Cora regarded them in silent amazement for some time, but she obviously realised how she had been duped, for she was never 'had' that way again.

Normally if Solomon was on my shoulder in the car and I had to enter some public place, I would leave him sitting on the rear view mirror, or pop him back into his travel cage, now always kept in the car for a convenient seed and water supply on any journey. On one occasion, however, Solomon had been so good and quiet that I forgot he was on my shoulder, and left the car with him still sitting there. Fortunately this happened at Farmers Market, the one spot in Hollywood/Los Angeles where an unusual sight was commonplace and therefore aroused no special reaction from its masses of shoppers and sightseers. Actually the sight of a parrot being given a shoulder ride was something that regular customers had become used to, for Bud, the pet shop owner, frequently carried one of his pets around in this manner. Solomon, however, did not care for the crowded surroundings, and after climbing on to my head in search of a perch on which he felt secure, eventually found his way to the centre of my bosom, where he hid, grumbling, 'twixt me and my dress 'til we returned to the car.

Since Solomon so clearly disliked shoulder-riding in a crowd, I thereafter ascertained that he was returned to his travel cage before accompanying me in similar circumstances. It was certainly the only time he appreciated this contraption, or rather preferred it to my shoulder and stayed in voluntarily. On other rare occasions when he happened to be shut in it, he picked with great determination at the catch, until its door came open. Then, with a shriek of delight, he would fly over to me, seeming justifiably proud of his efforts.

Chapter 3
Desert Travellers

When Solomon had been with me for six months I obtained a sizeable contract to decorate an hotel in Scottsdale, Arizona, in association with an excellent artist Baron Fritz von Drieberg, whose work graces many a maharajah's palace. Naturally this meant moving down there. My Hungarian friends who had worked on several jobs with me, decided to come too. Julius being an inventor as well as an excellent cabinet-maker, while Clara was skilled in such crafts as lampshade-making, we had between us a happy and useful working partnership.

For almost a week we lived in chaos, as the upheaval of packing up two homes and a workshop was sorted out. Finally at 5 a.m. one summer morning, encumbered by two U-Haul trailers, we began the great trek South in a car, a station-wagon and a 'Chevvy' truck, taking turns to drive the various vehicles. Solomon, agitated and grumbling was restless in his travel cage, while Suzy and her newly acquired pet, a stray cat, were no less put out by our early start. So we put all three together in the back of the station-wagon, with the purpose of having one rather than two, irritable drivers. But thankfully at the outset of our journey there was none, for all of them were soon fast asleep, Suzy and her cat curled uncomfortably around Solomon's cage.

We stopped for a hearty truckers' breakfast at Indio, a sea-level community in the midst of California's attractive date-growing oasis, and as usual were amused by the colourful language used by its waiting staff, which is peculiar to most such establishments. For instance, when someone aked for 'Coffee hot and sweet', the kitchen received an order for 'Coffee like a woman!', while a request for *'Chilli con Carne'* was translated to 'One bowl of Mexican heartburn'.

Eventually, invigorated by our meal, we once more set forth on our journey. Actually the advantage of our early start in avoiding heavy commuter traffic around Los Angeles, was heavily outweighed by the subsequent disadvantage of meeting the noon-day sun at the centre of the Mojave Desert, the discomfort being all the more severe because we were quite unprepared for it and none of our vehicles was air-conditioned. Meanwhile, refreshed by their nap, Suzy and both animals began their anticipated harassment of the station-wagon's consecutive drivers, so that each of us was hard put to it to complete our stint without nerves becoming frayed. It was because of their unsociable behaviour that we decided to forgo the somewhat doubtful pleasure of visiting Shields Date Gardens, four miles west of Indio, for the purpose of viewing a free thirty-minutes colour film on 'The Sex Life of Dates'!

I was the second driver to take the wagon in our planned relay system, handing over the truck plus U-Haul trailer to Clara who went ahead, while Julius brought up the rear in my Olds-mobile, which had the second trailer on tow. During my stint I had Suzy's ball find my head a suitable bouncing-off post a greater number of times than was good for my equanimity. Meanwhile the cat somersaulted after imaginery butterflies and exhibited an astonishing fixation for desiring to leap through the steering wheel at the most awkward moments. Solomon, perhaps because of the cat, chose to remain confined in his cage, yet proclaimed disapproval of his cramped discomfort in a manner excruciatingly painful to one's ear-drums. At the same time he twanged vigorously at the cage bars, until in this way he succeeded in snapping two, which was no mean feat, and left a gap quite large enough for him to have made his exit had he not been able to open its door, or indeed elected to continue his lamented confinement.

My sanity, strange to relate, was saved by a near disaster, although the consequences of it too were tiresome. I had been about to overtake a small car with preponderous caravan on tow, when Kitty, eager for more acrobatics around the steering wheel, leapt on to my lap. Fortunately his behaviour curtailed my intended manoeuvre, for as soon as I had pulled back behind the caravan, it began a violent 'fishtail' swerving back and forth across the narrow road. Suddenly it nose-dived against the tow-bar, somersaulted in mid-air, then crashed on its side, lying spread-eagled across our path, which forced me to swerve off the road, ploughing into the surrounding sand.

We might well have been under that unfortunate caravan and if the wagon had had one of the U-Hauls on tow it could also have been a more serious story, but luckily, although shaken, Suzy, Solomon, the cat and I were otherwise O.K. Yet our escape was not without its problems since the front of our car had become so deeply embedded in sand that I was quite unable to open its doors. Passengers of a coach, that had been travelling towards the crashed vehicles, were not so fortunate for the bus came to a violent halt a mere hair's-breadth from the blockage, giving many of its occupants bloody noses.

The road, by then impassable, was far too narrow for the coach to turn and get help from Blythe, which in any case was some eighty miles off. Julius, however, was not far behind and soon had the U-Haul unhitched from my Olds', which he turned without trouble and sped back towards Indio seeking assistance and taking with him the hysterically shocked elderly male driver of the tow car:

Meanwhile, in the period before help arrived, the station-wagon became oven-like, so with Suzy's help inside, along with that of the coach driver and a brawny passenger outside, we cleared a way to the tail-gate and got it open. From there we made our way into what shade there was, thrown by the coach. Since its air-conditioning had become defunct, most of its passengers sheltered there also, in the hope of catching an odd breeze. Suzy was carried over; just as well, since the sizzling sand scorched through my sandles to the soles of my feet, yet I found this preferable to the heat which had built up inside the car.

Sand dunes were sparsely scattered by scraggy Joshua trees, one of the oldest plants in American deserts, whose fibrous leaves are used by Red Indians for making cord, cloth and even a type of moccasin. Occasionally a tumbleweed blew prettily by and I collected one since they had many decorative uses. I also spotted the odd lizard and several times we heard the tell-tale rattle of the snakes so named. Yet although we heard them, none of us saw any, but in any event these distractions helped to pass the time while we waited for assistance.

Suzy, amazingly good, took our misadventure in her stride, enjoying the attention of coach passengers, who plied her with coke and fruit. It was Suzy's fat black cat and Solomon who gave cause for some concern, the breathing of both being laboured. The cat finally flaked out beneath the coach, while Solomon sat on my hand with little more energy, his eyes half shut and wings slightly raised. In spite of the crowd I had taken him out of the cage, having burnt my hand on its metal and thereby realized it was radiating extra heat upon him.

I felt water would diminish Solomon's obvious discomfort, but my efforts to make him drink proved fruitless, until I pretended to drink from his cup, at which point he surprised me by suddenly shoving his beak into my mouth and drinking my saliva. Since Solomon, though for no apparent reason, so clearly shunned his drinking water, I emptied it over him hoping this would help to cool him down. He was, however, quite unappreciative of this treatment, which was strange considering his usual partiality to being wet. Conversely the cat, whom I had expected to protest, took to his soaking without so much as a flick of his tail.

The sheriffs, in convoy with Julius and breakdown trucks, arrived shortly after 11.30 a.m. While Suzy, Solomon and the cat recovered their sensibilities waiting in one of the air-conditioned Hi-way patrol cars, the sheriffs took statements and supervised the work of the breakdown trucks in clearing the obstruction and digging out our car. They then obligingly supplied water, with which I was able to soak a number of towels, some of which I swathed around the cage. The same was done with a hastily constructed container for the cat, and once on the move this 'Heath Robinson' form of air-conditioning proved amazingly adequate. As for Suzy, Julius and myself, we kept a damp towel on our heads and around our shoulders. These too were relatively effective, staying moist to within a few miles of Desert Centre.

Desert Centre, aptly named, was the only form of habitation to be found in the ninety-seven miles comprising California's section of the Colorado Desert between Indio on its perimeter and Blythe state line. The township boasted no more than half-a-dozen or so ramshackle wooden huts, a one-pump garage, the inevitable souvenir shop, a cafe, a six-room motel, a post office, some caravans for the 'natives' and a hi-way patrol station. At the latter we met up with an anxious Clara who had been intercepted by the sheriffs there and so informed of our unavoidable delay.

Having refreshed ourselves at the cafe and replenished necessary water supplies we again got under way, this time keeping in closer convoy. Our appearance must have presented a strange sight – our inventive cooling system giving us the guise of 'amateur theatrical' Arabs. But at least our 'costume' was appropriate to a sandy desert – and its effectiveness more than compensated for the jeering toots of those passing motorists who felt superior in mechanically air-conditioned cars. Perhaps they thought we were practising for Indio's Arabian Nights-style Date Festival!

During a stop for 'high tea' at Arizona's central desert town of Salome, we noticed a considerable increase in wind force and hadn't been long on our way once again when it started 'whistling Dixie' (an American expression for the screaming howl of winds approaching hurricane force!). The sky blackened as eddies of sand spiralled upwards. Our cars rocked violently, even at an enforced standstill when the road had become completely blotted from view. Sand 'hailed' against the cars, pitting both paintwork and windscreens. Inside it was pitch dark, stifling and uncomfortably gritty for sand somehow penetrated the tightly shuttered windows.

Happily the sandstorm did not last long, the worst being over within twenty minutes, but it left us with considerable expenses for replacing windscreens and carrying out necessary engine cleans. We also had the more immediate predicament of being on an un-named road, or perhaps 'road' is too sophisticated a word for describing the rough earth track, crossing the Harquahala Plain, upon which we found ourselves, as we had accidentally kept too far to the right in following signpost directions to Phoenix, when leaving Salome in the gathering storm. Weird atmospheric effects as the sandstorm subsided made it easy to credit reports of people seeing Ghost Camels wandering the desert with skeleton riders. Camels had in fact been imported from Arabia, for desert use, by the Federal Army in its infancy, but for some reason both the camels and their native drivers had quickly died off. A memorial near Indio recalls their fatal brief sojourn.

It was so difficult to detect where the track actually was that we were fortunate to see a truck-load of bap-faced, lanky-haired, but friendly Red Indians held up not too far distant from where we had 'ridden out' the sandstorm. They were Pima Indians, clothed in unattractive adaptations of western dress, en route to their reservation at Gila-Bend, where we followed them. Pima Indians (River Dwellers) descendants of the pre-Columbian Hohokam culture, are basically corn farmers, but they make good use of Arizona's giant Saguaro cactus, employing its flowers and fruit for food, while water vessels and building materials are made from its stem. They also use fibres of the yucca in weaving their distinctive basketry, some of which we bought when parting company with them at Buckeye, less than thirty miles from our destination. We were, incidentally, pleasantly surprised to find on arrival at Phoenix that by following this unconventional route we had saved a good many miles.

Within the week we were settled into both house and studio, set on the edge of a citrus grove, whose trees bore a seemingly endless supply of truly luscious grapefruit. Happily we were allowed to help ourselves to as many as we liked, so grapefruit, both raw and cooked, became part of our staple diet. The next six weeks or so were spent working far into the night, to complete the items needed to refurnish the restaurant, convention rooms and lobby of Scottsdale's fashionable 'Safari' hotel, we'd contracted to decorate before their 'winter' season, which was after all the reason for our journey.

It was also the reason why during this time Solomon got less attention than I liked to give him. Even so his friendliness grew, as did his partiality for drinking from my mouth; yet this happened only when we were out of doors, or in car or truck, and lasted only for two to three months, when he returned, as at other times, to full use of more conventional sources of water!

Soon after we had completed the decorative installation work at the hotel my mother came out for a long visit. Solomon was able to manage short flights by then and as soon as Mother crossed the threshold, he flew straight on to her shoulder – the first time he had flown, in a completely voluntary manner, to anyone. So it was indeed a thrilling moment. He stayed on her shoulder while we had coffee, during which time he grabbed part of a sesame cracker and, having carefully eaten off its tiny seeds, rapidly demolished the then unwanted biscuit by flinging crunched-up pieces wildly around him, many of the crumbs becoming uncomfortably lodged between one's dress and person. He was definitely showing-off, hopping from Mother's shoulder to the back of her chair, quickly returning to biff her cheek, chattering excitedly and making sure he had her full attention. When I put out a hand for him, Solomon shook his head, saying 'No' very clearly before scrambling round the back of my mother's neck. Peeping at me from the far side he again said 'No', giving another defiant shake of his head! He seemed fascinated by this new-found word (his first) and the laughter it occasioned, for he repeated it with growing enthusiasm before returning to his cage and trying it out in front of his mirror.

Solomon would have nothing to do with me the rest of that day – shaking his head and saying 'No' until the time came for his goodnight 'handshake' and 'Radio Kiss' noises. Until that night I had been the only person whose hand he permitted in the cage after he was ready for sleep, giving nasty bites to anyone else who dared invade his 'bedroom'. On this occasion, however, he not only allowed Mother to put her hand in, he laid one foot on her index finger and gave it a gentle squeeze with his claws. This was indeed a sign of acceptance, for hitherto he had reserved this touchingly affectionate gesture solely for me.

Although Solomon was by then capable of short flights, he was unable to sustain them and could only 'take off' from some high object, so that if he landed on the ground he would stay there and proceed by walking to his destination. He did just this the morning after my mother's arrival. Talking in one of the bed-rooms, we became aware of the scratchy pitter-patter of Solomon's feet crossing the stone paved hallway as he came in search of us. He followed my guiding whistles and we were soon greeted to his comically inquiring head gazing up at us from round the door-way. 'Hullo Solomon,' said Mother; 'Solomon' he repeated, and shrieking joyfully, ran the few yards to the bed, quickly climbed its spread, and fluttered over to the dressing table. There he strutted up and down while he rehearsed his vocabulary of both parrot and human language, including a hilarious imitation of the spluttering regurgitations and backfires made by our lawn mower that was always a brute to start. From the lawn mower these noises were bad enough, but repeated by Solomon they sounded positively vulgar!

During my mother's stay, and largely due to her patient efforts, Solomon became much more venturesome in his eating habits. Although I knew that many parrots were basically fruit eaters, I had been unable to get Solomon to take any. This surprised me because I had assumed that the messy state his feathers were in when I got him was partly due to the sticky, staining juice of the 'parrot fruit' and was therefore at a loss to comprehend his rejection of other pulpy fruits. He also assiduously flung grapes, corn and nuts out of his seed dish as if they were repugnant foreign bodies – much as we might treat a caterpillar found in a salad! My Mother's early efforts in this direction had also proved 'fruitless' until one day she was gently stroking his bosom with a longish piece of apple peel, when he made a sudden grab for it. He flung the first piece aside, but its flavour had obviously got through, for he snatched the remainder and began avidly scraping flesh from skin. The next day while Mother was eating some seedless grapes she offered one to Solomon who was sitting on her shoulder. This too he took and ate with apparent relish. Since that day he has graciously accepted most fruit offered to him.

Our sojourn in Arizona was possibly one of the happiest times of Solomon's life since he was able to have a great deal of outdoor freedom there and the terrain was the closest to that of his natural habitat that we ever lived in. In late afternoons, when pleasantly warm breezes tempered the sun's rays and Mother and I sat relaxing on the verandah, Solomon spent many long hours climbing happily about the garden's one and only orange tree. Occasionally he flew over to one of us to say a brief 'Hullo', or went to his cage, left outside for most of the day, to get a drink or some seeds, but it was never long before he would return to the orange tree and sit busily preening amongst its lower branches. Then as the sun set he would climb higher and higher, as if to watch its final dip below the horizon. He often looked pensive at these times and I wondered if he was thinking longingly of his congeners, but after the sun had set completely and the chirrups of cicadas began he would start agitating for a chair-lift indoors. Occasionally we waited to see if he would settle down in the tree for the night, but he never did, and having fluttered down from its boughs began in a panic-strciken way to wander about the scrubby grass until one of us went near. Then hopping on to the nearest shoe, he would peck at one's ankle until he was lifted shoulder high and returned ceremoniously to his cage.

A lively roadrunner

Sometimes in the early evening he would be startled by the sudden appearance of two Jack Rabbits living in the garden, but mostly his hours out of doors were peaceful for none of the really wild birds ever bothered Solomon while he played in the orange tree, possibly because most of them chose various cacti, liberally lining the perimeter of our compound, for their habitat. Nevertheless the friendliest of these birds – and the ones that to me evoke Arizona more than any other – the lively, inquisitive roadrunners, often surrounded Solomon when he was on the verandah, shut inside his cage. At these times there was great competition amongst the roadrunners as regards making off with food which Solomon was wont to fling at them although, since they were mainly insect and lizard eaters, I have no idea what they actually did with their spoils. The roadrunners showed no fear when Mother or I went near. They knew the car and always welcomed us back from an outing by running alongside it as we drove up to the house. We became very fond of these lively clowns of the desert, and this was not only because they kept snakes, scorpions and the like at bay.

It was after one of Solomon's 'socials' with the roadrunners that we noticed him biting, rather than preening his feathers. This developed, with horrifying rapidity, into self-disfigurement, as he stripped his bosom bare. It was, we assumed, a case of mites and we hastily purchased a spray designed to kill them, to be used on both bird and cage. Easier said than done as far as Solomon was concerned. He did not 'Go' for this treatment one little bit. In the end we were forced to catch hold of him and while Mother held him, spreading open each wing in turn, I sprayed. He was extremely cross by the time we had finished and for quite a while would have nothing to do with either of us.

Directions on the anti-mite spray read: (a) Thoroughly spray bird and cage with disinfectant. (b) Set bird to dry. (c) Thoroughly spray bird with clean, warm water. – Back to square one! – Neither Mother nor I fancied the idea of spraying him again since he'd so obviously disliked it, and out of sheer perverseness it was unlikely that he would give himself a bath. So by the time the mite spray had dried, giving his feathers a dull, powdery appearance, we had decided to wash him in a basin. There again this was easier thought of than done, for he was still so annoyed that I had to resort to the use of gloves to get him to come to me. However once he had been dumped in the basin of water and Mother began splashing some on his back he gave up his struggles and being resigned to his fate offered no further resistance. Eventually we had him so completely waterlogged that he was quite unable to move, even if he had wanted to and he sat, eyes closed, in the palm of my hand looking pathetically like a drowned vulture fledgling.

Since it was fairly late in the day when the above hoo-ha took place we turned on one of the hot air blowers to help dry him off, which even so took some time to achieve. In the intervening period Solomon kept dozing off, swaying precariously on the back of a chair. Eventually, when dry, he still remained disgruntled and refused peace-offerings of titbits, from both Mother and myself. Happily he was his usual cheerful self the next morning.

The following weekend being particularly humid I decided to take a tepid mid-day shower. Solomon was in the bathroom at the time gazing intently out of the window at a black labrador wandering in the citrus grove. But no sooner had I started my shower than Solomon began showing the same excitement that he had exhibited on hearing the dolphin fountain. It was not long before he flew over to my shoulder, digging his claws painfully deep into my bare skin. At first he spread and flapped his wings in excitement, but in the end he sat quite still, eyes closed in sheer contentment. After that day it was difficult to keep him away from the shower and he often joined me there, but, expecting him, I kept a towel round my shoulders to prevent undue scratching.

Later than same afternoon, whilst sitting in the orange tree to dry off, he started shrieking in a way that meant 'Stranger in camp'. Mother and I were sunbathing and opened our eyes to see the black labrador sniffing around the base of Solomon's tree. It was thin and wore no collar and although we shooed it off to the citrus grove a couple of times, it kept coming back. To cut a long story short, we later found that it had been abandoned by some fruit pickers and was therefore a stray. Feeling sorry for the dog, we began putting scraps out for it, but it wasn't long before 'Negra' had wormed his way into our household. Like Solomon he was fond of a shower, and also made full use of the bath tub to sleep in, finding it a suitably cool spot on hot summer nights. There Negra generally made a ridiculous sight, for his chosen attitude was to lie on his back, legs waving aimlessly in the air.

Actually Negra turned out to be quite a clown, and was always up to some sort of mischief, the results of which were often quite comical. Once, for instance, he gulped down a quantity of green glitter that I was using to decorate some gift items for a local boutique. I was aghast, but it did him no harm and that evening Mother Nature eliminated it from his system in her own particular way. It was, of course, rather spectacular and several passersby stopped to exclaim in amazement at Negra's sparkling green excreta. 'It's Stardust,' was my tongue-in-cheek answer to their enquiries, indicating that Negra was just back from outer space! Of course I had a very hard time trying to keep a straight face when my explanation was accepted, but since there was, in fact, a

The magnificent "Queen Mary" was Solomon's five day home on his voyage to England

Studying reflections

A mutual admiration society

space research base in the vicinity, the gullibility of these onlookers was perhaps understandable.

Three weeks later, with Mother's six months visa drawing to a close, we decided to take a short trip to Mexico. Solomon was far from being fit to return to his native land for he had begun to moult, which adversely affected his power of flight, so we left him and Negra with Clara for the few days we were away. During our return journey we stopped the car for a while to take photographs of the hauntingly beautiful but deserted Apache Trail. It was some hours since we had passed a car or seen any sign of human habitation. Imagine our surprise, therefore, when on returning to our convertible we found a pretty Alsatian bitch, sprawled out on the back seat. We tried cajoling her out of the car, but she just whimpered and stayed put. Then we noticed her torn pads and burr-matted coat; obviously she had travelled some distance. It seemed incredible that anyone could have abandoned such a delightful pup, but there was the tell-tale lack of collar, which normally carries licence number and identification of the owner. Hoping that someone would turn up to claim her, we stayed there for our picnic lunch, most of which was wolfed by the dog, who then fell into an exhausted sleep. Eventually we drove to the nearest Highway Patrol headquarters to find out if any such dog had been reported missing; none had.

The sheriff then told us that an appalling number of pets were abandoned each year, mainly by elderly couples who retire to desert climes only to find they miss their city lights, and for some incomprehensible reason, instead of finding homes for their newly acquired pets – who are not suited to apartment living – they leave them to die of starvation in the desert. 'Lucky' ones, found wandering by police are humanely destroyed, if homes are not found for them within three days. I hated to think of this beautiful puppy ending in the gas chamber – after all, what was one more dog? Thus 'Queenie' joined the household. It was a sad day for all of us when the time came for my Mother's departure and in spite of the animals, the house seemed very empty after she had gone, so I was glad to have a great deal of work in hand.

During my Mother's visit and the ten months following it I was kept busy decorating boutiques, restaurants and bars, in many varied styles, both plain and fancy, ranging from Moroccan, German Hoffbrau, Chinese, Parisian and Provincial, to blatantly

Sexy. In sharp contrast there was an interesting 90-foot bank mural depicting the history of Arizona, and an assignment to make some experimental scenic backgrounds for 'Houses' of the local zoo's smallest mammals.

The Arizona Zoo, then in its infancy, was not at that time the formal institution that most large ones necessarily become. Therefore I spent many delightful hours playing with the tamer beasts, such as a magnificent cheetah, presented by a Persian Princess. On two occasions I took Solomon up to the Zoo with me. The director in charge of general development expressed surprise at finding him so friendly, saying that in his experience these particular conures were extremely difficult to tame. Solomon was on his shoulder at the time of the remark, which however was made before he disgraced himself by biting the director's ear after I had teasingly twigged his tail! But I must say this incident was taken in good part. Actually I have come across other Petz's Conures far tamer than Solomon – one, for instance, who was trained to ride a toy scooter and do other tricks, much as India's Senegals entertain in the bazaar – and Sheba is certainly far sweeter natured, while others I know have borne out the director's theory of aggression. I can only assume this diversity arises because of the immensely individual characters that these little fellows possess, although possibly this also has something to do with the age at which they are caught, as an untamed adult Petz's can be an extremely unpleasant adversary.

Personally, I have always felt pleased that although Solomon's attachment to me was undoubtedly genuine and strong, it was but that of a fledgling for its parent. Thus when Sheba eventually came into his life, he was able quite naturally to transfer his affection to her and settle down so well to what we all hope will be joyful parenthood, at London Zoo; unlike some disillusioned parrots, such as one particular Hyacinthine Macaw in London Zoo, who pines for and delights in his keeper's petting, and sadly, is not the least interested in others of his species. Unfortunately in this instance the parrot would be far happier as a free and pampered family pet and I often long to bring him home for odd weekend holidays. Somehow I have become somewhat attached to this rather dissolute, handsome, old character who, to my mind quite understandably, destroys the bars of his cage as rapidly as they are replaced, and although he has a reputation for biting I personally have always found him to be extremely gentle and affectionate.

But I digress. Finally my work in Arizona came to an end. Julius and Clara returned to Los Angeles, while I travelled through New Mexico to continue my studies of Red Indian Art, but that again is another story. I need only mention here that Solomon's presence broke the ice on many occasions, for the Indians always welcomed him, and he on his part took to most of them.

From New Mexico I went on to Denver where I had three contracts lined up, all of which were referals from my work in Phoenix. There was, however, not much of note that happened in Denver as regards Solomon. He just got cheekier as time went by and demanded even more attention, which may have been due to jealousy regarding the dogs, although he got on well with them. More often than not, on evenings when I had time to relax, all three did their best to sit on my lap at the same time, each making sure he got his full share of affection and petting. So it was fortunate that the sofa I had at the time was large enough to take two spread-eagled dogs apart from myself and Solomon, who would often settle down on one of their heads.

I did not stay long in Denver, it being a town that took generally a somewhat dim view of animals, and in any case better prospects loomed tantalisingly from the direction of Chicago, so once more I packed up and took to the road. Here again I came across the fairly widespread American phobia of disliking even well-behaved animals in public places. In one state a law forbids transient animals to walk in the grounds of a motel, let alone its rooms, and insists that pets be boarded separately in kennels run specifically for this purpose; and deplorably inadequate they were too. The flapped-about principles of hygiene that seemed to be behind the aforementioned ban certainly hadn't penetrated the kennels I saw. Thus on three separate occasions I grabbed what sleep I could in a car loaded to the hilt, with a parrakeet and two dogs as my strangely assorted bedfellows.

Later, when it was too late to be of use, I discovered that 'Texaco' put out a guide, revised annually, of motels sensibly admitting pets. Well worth its 25 cents for anyone intending to travel across the U.S.A. with their pets in tow, it can be obtained from their head office in New York City.

Chapter 4

From Deep Freeze to Oven

Solomon busily removes lace from my nightdress

As has been seen Solomon, always a clean little bird, loves bathing, but unfortunately, on one occasion, this passion for getting wet was very nearly his end. It was soon after our arrival in Chicago, which had been heralded by severe weather conditions. When the temperature dropped rapidly to 15° below zero it was, I felt, far too cold to take Solomon to my atelier with its inadequate heating arrangements (one ancient radiator for 2,000 sq. ft.), so for the first time he was left alone. As circumstances turned out it would have been far better had I taken him.

By midday both dogs and myself were shivering, so for a quick remedy we took a run through the park, ending up near the apartment block. I decided to lunch there and incidentally see how Solomon was faring on his own. It was indeed fortunate that I did so as the communal central heating had broken down, therefore the building felt, if anything, colder than the 'great outdoors'.

On entering my apartment I was surprised to get no answering call to my whistle, but assumed Solomon was piqued at having been left behind. I was quite unprepared for the truly disastrous cause of his silence, because although I had naturally expected to find an extremely cold parrot, I had not expected to find a completely frozen one, and this is just what Solomon was! Apparently he had taken one of his 'grand' baths, then flown to the cross-bar of the living-room sash window, a cold, draughty spot at any time. On that particular day, however, there were icicles up to 6in. long hanging from this bar outside; nevertheless Solomon unwisely used it in preference to branches entwined on the top of his cage, where he had been sitting when I left.

When I found him he sat soaking wet and immobilised on the cross-bar, since, as I saw to my horror, the foot he rested on was literally frozen to the wood, while the icicles outside were matched by tiny icicles on his quivering bosom. Albeit, the pupils of his eyes contracted, as they always do when he sees me or gets excited about something.

Yet I was concerned to detect a harsh, croaky/clicking accompanying his laboured panting – a sound indicative of bronchitis or pneumonia, both of which I knew were likely to be fatal – but, for the time being he was still alive; thus although I felt that his end must surely be near, the faint hope of his possible survival drove me to quick, if limited, action.

Luckily there was a gas stove so, lighting all the jets for warmth, I heated water and dabbed this round Solomon's frozen foot, until I was able to lift him off. He offered not the least resistance to being handled in this unfamiliar way, nor was there any protest when I enveloped him loosely in cotton wool and a towel before popping him into the oven, on at its lowest setting, with the front open.

I stroked Solomon's head and massaged his icy beak for a long twenty minutes before he began to grumble and started agitating to get out of his, by then sodden, wrappings. He

53

remained passive while I removed them, although he had taken a firm hold of my index finger, giving it an occasional gentle chew. Great shivers began to rack his body as his grumbles became frantic. It was obvious that Solomon was in great pain as he thawed out, and it was heart-breaking not to be able to ease this in any positive way. Even the dogs, huddled nearby, began whimpering in distressed sympathy.

It suddenly struck me that food might help, not only to warm Solomon, but to take his mind off this unaccustomed discomfort. The sunflower seeds being within reach I offered him one which he immediately grabbed and flung aside. Then he gave me what was probably the nastiest bite of our acquaintance. No doubt this was his way of expressly blaming me for his misfortune! Happily Solomon's annoyance had the beneficial side effect of showing him he could move normally again. Thus, after another attempt at nipping me, he began knocking my hand with his beak, then a fit of sneezing putting an end to that, he started preening himself between shivers.

Seeing that Solomon was sufficiently recovered to stand on his own two feet, I settled him on the edge of the oven, before going off to tie up my badly bleeding finger. There were shrieks of protest and a flutter of wings as I left the room, but obviously he was too waterlogged to fly, because the next thing I knew, Queenie padded through with Solomon on her back. He made another attempt to fly but failed, landing with a thud at my feet, and began clambering awkwardly up my trousered leg. So it seemed that in spite of his grievance against me, he was not keen to let me out of his sight again, that day at least.

While in the living-room I 'phoned to Reception enquiring: 'How long before the heating is repaired?' The dismal answer: 'Not 'til late tomorrow, Ma'am' would, I felt, really put paid to Solomon's chances of survival, so I decided to move into a hotel for the night – no easy matter, since, as already mentioned, few hotels in the States will take pets. By then it was 3.40 p.m. and we had still had no lunch so, whilst telephoning around, I staved off the pangs of hunger with cheese. Because both Negra and Queenie loved cheese I shared it with them, absent-mindedly handing some to Solomon also. Surprisingly he took and ate it with apparent relish. This was the first time he had had any dairy product, and cheese in particular I would have thought he would dislike, if only in memory of his long, dark hours in the Taco bag.

Yet Solomon's liking for cheese grew and he is now quite a connoisseur, disdaining processed varieties, and savouring sharp Cheddars, Dunlop and even Camembert! This latter choice is unfortunate, since its odour is inclined to emanate from him for two or three days after its consumption. Actually, although he gets only minute, crumb-like portions, Solomon's intake of cheese is strictly rationed, since we noticed he becomes bad-tempered, as if livery, on consuming large quantities. Oddly enough, cooked cheese – supposedly more indigestible – is the exception, and a piece of macaroni or cauliflower cheese soon became firm favourites.

By 4 p.m. I had managed to book in at the luxurious Edgewater Beach Hotel, situated, as its name implies, on parkland over-looking Lake Michigan, lying between Chicago and Evanston. There was a genuine welcome from the staff at this pleasant hotel, for my menagerie, and on signing in I was handed an amusing card, greeting the dogs, that listed a host of human guest failings, ending up with the lines: 'Neither do you leave cigarette burns on the bed clothes, so welcome pooch, and if you can put up with your two-footed friend, so can we!'

Meanwhile Solomon, still wet and shivering, was huddled close into my neck and between sneezes held firmly on to my ear. It was with considerable difficulty that he was persuaded to enter his travelling cage. Once he was in I swathed the cage completely with two towels and an old coat, to act as a barrier to Chicago's biting winds, while transferring from building to car, etc. There was plenty of air for such a short journey but the dogs were not at all happy to have Solomon so enveloped and both were an utter nuisance, pawing at the bundle and whining until, having reached our allotted room at the hotel, I took the covers off. There they sniffed anxiously round the cage and once its door was open Negra unwisely stuck his nose in, much to Solomon's vexation, for he growled at Negra quite fiercely and then nipped his nose before the astonished dog had time to move out of the way. This was the first time I had heard Solomon growl. He has since done so only occasionally, but always for an appropriate reason.

It was as well that both dogs were good-natured, for Solomon's next attack was on the Alsatian. He had landed on her back again in another attempt to fly to me. Once there he used his beak as a battering-ram, knocking violently at her snout. Then, when I put my hand down for him, he naughtily gave her ear a quick sharp nip, before scrambling up my arm as fast as he could. Queenie just yawned, wagged her tail and went off to hog the radiator beside Negra.

Before I could join them there, there was a knock at the door. It was the manager's assistant who, having heard of Solomon's plight from the bell boy, had come to offer his help, and had been thoughtful enough to bring with him a fan-type heater to hasten the drying-off process. Thanks to this consideration – and to my great relief – this object was achieved in a relatively short space of time, since Solomon's sneezing and harsh croaking were distinctly worse. But even when his feathers were quite dry and his feet and beak were warm to the touch Solomon's body still quivered, so possibly he was suffering from shock. Strangely he seemed to like being held cupped in my hands while I petted him. Previously he had always objected if I had tried handling him in a familiar way. Since his recovery, however, he has been distinctly more friendly, often demanding that his head feathers be ruffled, but except for the first few weeks after Sheba joined our household (to begin with he was jealous of her) he has never again been quite so permissive.

After he had had nearly an hour of petting on the evening of his 'big freeze' I tried him with food once more. This time he sat quite still in my lap, looking very sorrowful, holding the seed in his beak but making no attempt to crack it open. To encourage him, I cracked one; he dropped his, took the shelled one very gently and ate slowly, a faraway expression in his eyes. I then continued shelling seeds until he had had his fill. When Solomon finished eating he refused water from his cup. Instead he clambered up to my shoulder, agitating to drink from my mouth as he had done in the desert. I am not normally given to pampering animals but, as on the previous occasion, I felt conditions now justified it. From then on, however, it became a habit I was unable to break him of, until the arrival of Sheba, that is.

It was only after many hours of petting that Solomon was persuaded to return to his cage, which I had put partially covered on the bed-side table, with the fan heater behind it. Once in he settled down to sleep fairly quickly. As for myself, I got very little 'shut-eye' that night, being anxious about him, although by the early hours his breathing was more or less normal again. Our room became stifling with the extra heat, but I kept the blower on, being convinced that this was what really saved Solomon, so any discomfort I felt was well worth the miracle of his survival.

Nevertheless it was a relief when the chamber-maid brought tea up at 7 a.m. next morning. She enquired kindly after Solomon, asked when I would like breakfast and said the bell-boy was waiting to take the dogs out. The friendly staff all continued to be most helpful, giving thoughtful, quick and efficient service, taking the dogs for their requisite number of outings, feeding them with so-called 'kitchen scraps' and bringing my own meals up to our room. So since it was a Sunday with no business commitments arranged we were fortunately able to have a fairly quiet day.

I enjoyed the luxury of breakfast in bed. Solomon watched me sleepily for a while, then quite suddenly flew to the edge of the tray, regaling me with his greeting call. He briefly permitted his head to be stroked then, after banging a plate with his beak, hopped on to my shoulder, there giving my cheek a few sharpish pecks. We quizzed each other for some moments before he started 'showing off', first by stretching each wing slowly out, revealing the true beauty of their colours, then flapping them vigorously. At the end of this performance he poked his beak into my mouth, obviously looking for food. Trying not to encourage him in that particular method of obtaining it, I put him back in the cage beside his feed cups; he knocked crossly on them, shrieking in fury and, when I laughed, began using his beak as a shovel, flinging seeds out of their containers and scattering them to the far corners of the room – which display of temperament took hours to clear up. But, just as suddenly as he had started this Hoo-ha he stopped, flew once more to my shoulder with a seed in his beak and, after biffing it against my cheek, dropped it down the neck of my nightdress. Then, giving me more greeting calls, he rubbed his head under my chin in a thoroughly soppy manner. It was quite impossible to resist such an endearing appeal so, of course, Solomon had his way and ate a large, hand-fed breakfast.

As I have already said, Solomon has been markedly more friendly since his aforementioned ordeal. Quite understandably, he now also shows a great dislike of being left alone. Coupled with this he becomes noticeably annoyed if left out of any activity going on around him. It was not often that either of these situations occurred, but should they do so he made his disapproval quite clear in one of two ways. Either he would sulk and turn huffily away when eventually spoken to, or alternatively, he resorted to the more positive and expensive reaction of chewing things. This latter was indubitably his preferred form of protest, and as it happened he got into practice that very night.

Around 7 p.m. Solomon had left my shoulder, of his own accord, to eat in his cage, instead of demanding to be hand fed, which made me decide to take the dogs out personally. They enjoyed playing in the snow so much, as I too enjoyed the fresh air after my voluntarily overheated confinement of the past thirty-six hours, that I stayed out longer than intended. On arriving back in our room I found Solomon at the foot of the bed determinedly removing the Liberty's label from a mohair travel rug an aunt had given me – no more free advertising for them! The long hairs kept tickling him, so one foot was kept active as he scratched himself. Since at the same time he was tugging vigorously at the stitching, he eventually overbalanced, flew with what dignity he could muster to his cage and became quite abusive.

Obviously Solomon was well on the road to complete recovery, even so I felt an early night would do him no harm, so as soon as he entered his cage for a liberal drink – chewing mohair rugs being thirsty work – I covered it, as on the previous evening, with an old towel. At this he went quickly to his bed perch and waved his 'paw' for a goodnight handshake. He settled down so well I took dinner downstairs, first shutting the cage door to ensure there would be no repeat foray on the rug.

I was gone, I suppose, not more than half-an-hour, but on return found a sizeable pile of towelling on the cage floor, and two holes in its cover which, of course, Solomon could reach quite easily through the bars. 'You bad bird,' I said, opening the cage door, but Solomon, choosing to ignore this mild admonishment, gave me another goodnight handshake and was sound asleep within ten minutes, his head tucked cosily underneath his wing.

In my early consciousness next morning I become aware of a strange noise, such as a serrated knife would make cutting something brittle, while my shoulder felt uncomfortably like a pin-cushion. Awakening properly I found Solomon upon it, his claws dug firmly in, grumbling and tugging away at the neckline of my nightdress; thread was making cobwebs around his head – hence his grumbles. The wretch, being a really early bird, and having woken to find me still asleep, had amused himself by busily removing the many rows of lace around my nightie! I have to admit, however, the job was so neatly done that even an ex-perienced tailor could not have bettered it, neither lace nor night-dress being torn.

We stayed a full week at the Edgewater Beach. Although initially expensive this sojourn did in fact prove beneficial to all. Solomon recovered completely and revelled in loads of attention from a great many people. I got orders for murals at two nearby motels (the hotel manager, having seen samples of my work in my room, had pre-sold its merits to the owners of the motels in question). As for the dogs, they both got good permanent homes out of our stay. Of course I was sorry to part with them, but I had decided to return to England and felt for several reasons they would be better off left in America.

Both couples taking the dogs had children and weekend country 'cabins', which was naturally an ideal set-up for them, and happily both dogs settled quickly into their new homes. More immediately, they were able to enjoy running directly into a park without the palaver of getting them to wear their boots through the streets, then getting their circulation back to normal, since the necessarily tight straps most certainly affected this.

Originally I had thought snow-boots for dogs was just one more example of commercialistic pandering to the sentimentally mis-guided instincts of many pet owners. I found just how wrong I was and just how much of an evil necessity these boots were only after hearing Queenie and Negra squeal with pain, caused by harsh chemicals put down to dissolve snow and ice on the 'side-walk'. Actually the first few times they wore boots the dogs were a truly comical sight, for they could not keep their balance or walk straight, and acted rather like new-born foals. Nevertheless, even when they got used to these encumbrances, the boots were not appreciated and had to be kept well out of reach when off, for they had become their most desired object with which to indulge in a tug-of-war.

Although from then on Solomon grumbled during most of the hours we spent at the apartment it seemed strangely quiet without the dogs. Happily our time there was minimal since the work I had come to do in Chicago was nearing completion, so all of the daylight hours and much of the night too were spent in the chilly workshop. Solomon kept me company suffering no ill effect except for getting icy cold extremities, and even that was not for long because he soon discovered that sitting on my shoulder was an adequate way of keeping his feet warm. Thus he deserted his hitherto favourite perch on the spray lines.

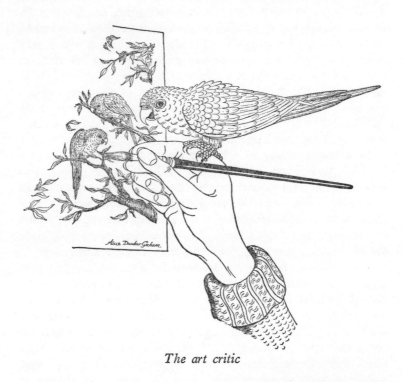

The art critic

Much as I enjoyed his company there, he was a distraction and occasionally he hampered the progress of my work for if he felt I was not giving him enough attention he would scamper down my arm, grabbing at the pencil or paintbrush being used, then proceed to demolish it at great speed in some spot where he was well out of reach. Possibly it was some form of jealousy. At other times he would sit for hours on my hand, watching intently as the painting took shape. Sometimes he voiced approval of what he saw, but at other times he would quizz me, a look of sheer amazement on his face, give a few disgusted grunts, as if to say, 'I could have done better than that myself,' and take off to pursue a more stimulating occupation than that of Art Critic.

On the day of installation I again risked leaving Solomon alone in the apartment to pursue his own devices, having first got an assurance from the manageress that she would call me should anything untoward happen to the building's essential services. Apart from getting in the way on these occasions, Solomon always became very nervous when present during installations, being for some reason afraid of workmen carrying long poles or ladders. Why this should be so I do not know. To hazard a guess, it could be something to do with the way he was caught.

It was an exhausting day and I arrived back late, but Solomon greeted me affectionately, flying over before I had the door fully open. Having poured myself a drink I sat him on my knee and spent a relaxing half hour ruffling his feathers. There was an ominous dusting of fabric fluff on them, but on looking round I could see nothing he might have chewed, until, that is, I drew the curtains. One was O.K., but the other was only half its correct length! So Solomon, it seemed, had been as busy as I that day! Sitting on the ledge where he had frozen, he had vented his spleen by chewing the curtains in two in an almost perfectly straight line, so that I was able, incidentally, to tack the bottom piece back without too much difficulty.

After the above incident I felt it was perhaps as well that our stay in that apartment was nearly over. We did in fact leave it on the following Monday, having first spent the weekend enjoying a happy reunion with Queenie and the Khalman family, her new owners, at their log cabin in Wisconsin.

My work in central Chicago complete, we moved back into the Edgewater Beach for a further week whilst completing the motel mural work. Again my stay there proved fortuitous for I met the head of a Tennessee motel group and, having signed a contract with him, left for 'Hillbilly' country the following week.

Solomon, sensing that we were leaving the snow and cold for sun and warmth, perhaps by the sight of our car piled high with luggage and equipment, seemed as pleased as I to be deserting the 'Windy City'. He sat happily on my shoulder, making his contented rasping noises, stopping them only to growl, quite fiercely, at any offending traffic light that dared to hold us up!

Chapter 5

Snake-killer Wild

A 'Domeliner' train enters canyon country

My assignment in Memphis was to design a series of simple murals for printing on vinyl wallpaper to use in bedrooms of motels owned by the 'combine' that commissioned me. Apparently the cost of putting even one widely reproduced print in these rooms had become prohibitive, since light-fingered paying guests steadily removed them – as they did with any other easily lifted fitments.

Anticipating correctly that the work would not take long I stayed at the motel where the company had its headquarters. One afternoon I was giving Solomon an outing at the back of the motel on a seldom used patch of grass, when his attention was caught by a garden hose. He eyed it with suspicion and thereafter jumped nervously at the least sound or movement of trees in the breeze. Since he appeared not to be enjoying this outing I had turned to go in when the hose leapt and twisted madly to and fro. Someone had obviously turned the water on with full force. Solomon gave a terrified cry and shot off. He landed briefly in a tree, then flew downward into a rough field whose arundinaceous grasses came up to my waist. Having followed Solomon's flight path I vaguely knew the spot where he had landed; even so it would be like looking for a needle in a haystack, unless he made a noise to guide me. This was unlikely, for when badly frightened he stretched his body tautly upright, remained stock-still, not even blinking an eye, and kept as silent as a taxidermist's specimen.

At that moment there chanced to occur one of life's strange coincidences. A loaded station-wagon pulled up at a nearby cabin, its occupants none other than the family who had taken Queenie to its heart! In a remarkably short space of time Solomon's disappearance had been explained to them and Queenie requested to 'Seek'. In less than three minutes a triumphant, deep-throated 'Woof' announced Solomon's discovery. Queenie's bark was rapidly followed by a yelp and an indignant squawk as Solomon again took to the air, this time flying back to my shoulder. Queenie had unwisely tried to pick Solomon up, at least we assumed this, since she returned to us with a bleeding snout but proudly carrying two tail feathers, while Solomon's back showed traces of her saliva.

That evening the Khalmans and I had a boisterous reunion, spurred on with wild music supplied by an excellent 'Hill-Billy' band, and I arranged to join them at their Texas homestead on completion of my work in Memphis. It had been my intention to spend but a week in Texas, but on arrival I found that the Khalmans had kindly lined up a good three months' work for me. This mainly consisted of murals for friends of theirs living in and around the Dallas area. Thus, delaying my intended departure for Britain, I took an apartment on the residential outskirts of Dallas, with which I managed to rent a second garage for studio use. Conveniently the resident gardener did all the necessary installation work for me and I engaged his wife, Rosie as part-time cook/housekeeper.

Rosie, a typical 'Black Mammy', was as cheerful as she was abundant, with a child-like capacity for being amused by simple events. Rosie's benevolence, however, came to an abrupt end if ever she encountered Solomon. I think he must have mistaken her for the maid we had in Los Angeles. At any rate, on the

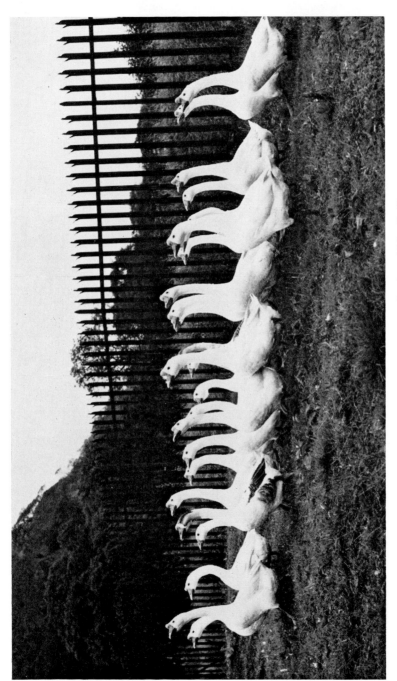

The gregarious "Scotch Guard" on duty at a Ballantine whisky distillery

Plenty of room to stretch a wing – Solomon in his airy aviary at London Zoo

Not quite Siamese twins – Solomon and Sheba at London Zoo

first morning that Rosie came to work, it was fortunate that I was still in the apartment, for just seconds after she entered the bedroom, where Solomon sat primping in front of the dressing-table mirror, there were shrieks from both. Rosie came rushing out, flapping a duster wildly about her head, which Solomon sat determinedly atop, savagely attacking her forehead, hand and duster. He fought fiercely as I got him off, but eventually I managed it, took him back to the bedroom and shut him in. His protest could be heard throughout the block. Initially it lasted a full twenty minutes and was thereafter repeated, at intervals, throughout the day.

Rosie was no less of a handful. On re-entering the living-room, I found her swigging liberally at a newly opened bottle of Haig & Haig. 'Missy Anne, wha's dat green devil you got in dare?' she asked, her eyes rolling and body shaking. I had to admit there were times when Solomon looked evil, but never had I suspected he could be such a virago!

It was hardly a fortuitous start to Rosie's working for me and in fact, that day, there was none done, for whisky soon had the effect of giving Rosie the shakes of a far different kind, and for nearly an hour my eyes were inflicted with the sight of Rosie performing a negro version of 'Knees up Mother Brown' before she fell into a drunken stupor on the sofa, where, clutching the then empty bottle, she snored the afternoon away. Thereafter I always made sure that Solomon was in the studio, or at any rate locked up, before Rosie arrived. In preference I kept him out of the apartment while Rosie was around, because if she did come in while he was caged, she delighted in taunting the 'Green Devil' and although Solomon retaliated as best he could, it was hardly a fair situation. Strangely Solomon never took the slightest notice of Rosie's husband.

At the workshop the spray-lines, which I had hooked up out of the way overhead, became his favourite perch. He stayed put there no matter who came in and whether or not I was using the spray, and amongst his usual chatter he began giving perfect imitations of the hissing made by pressurised air being released through the compressor's safety valve. In fact, though Solomon rarely used any human language, he became a great imitator of any odd sounds like this which caught his fancy.

While in Texas I generally spent the weekends with the Khalman family, and was not the only one to enjoy them. Solomon had taken a great liking to all their children and consequently put up with a great deal of handling from them. He particularly seemed to enjoy being taken for rides on the handlebars of one or other of their bicycles. Clinging tight with his claws, he slightly spread his wings for balance and chattered excitedly. Liking the children as he did, he occasionally grew tired of their company, and would then fly back into the coolly dim interior of their house, where he'd settle atop one of the many costly pictures that decorated each room and there, pressed close to the thick adobe walls, he would snatch a peaceful 'forty winks'. From that time on a picture frame has been Solomon's chosen perch whenever he has felt inclined to have an afternoon nap.

I was sorry to leave Texas, having found that the extravagant tales I'd heard, regarding the average 'Southerner's' warmhearted friendliness and hospitality were in no way exaggerated. But leave I must, my passage to England having finally been booked for the end of that summer, and I still had business to attend to in Los Angeles. The drive back there was over the familiar terrain of New Mexico and Arizona, where I stopped for a few days, staying with friends at their ranch a few miles from Phoenix.

The second evening we had just settled down on the verandah with long cool drinks, intending to enjoy the sunset, when there started from within the house a most terrible commotion. We rushed to the room where Solomon had been left to eat his supper in peace and found him repeatedly swooping down upon a small horned rattlesnake. The Parkers' dalmation was also attacking the hideous creature, which was leaping into the air. At the same time as the snake dived forward, it threw itself sideways, in an agile flaying movement. Its action was so fast it was difficult to follow, but actually that is the reason for this particular rattlesnake having 'sidewinder' as a nickname. Its descriptive common name horned rattlesnake is no less appropriate, referring as it does to the horn-like protrusions above its eyes. Its belly was fairly smooth and palish in colour, but its back and side scales were ridged, and although overall it was a brownish-yellow, there were scattered blotches of a deeper hue.

In spite of the snake's manoeuvres Solomon and the dalmation had killed it between them before we humans had time to take stock of the situation. The dog, having finally picked up the rattler near its head, shook it madly from side to side, and it was some considerable time before he could be persuaded to part with his prize. Later that same evening I cut off the snake's tail end, which houses its rattle, and, having skinned the piece, let it sun-dry the following day. It is now one of my prized souvenirs.

Solomon remained highly excitable the rest of that evening and although he stayed put on my shoulder, for a long time he kept jumping at the flickerings of the oil lamps (electricity had not quite reached the vast cactus-strewn acres of the Parker ranch). Even when I had him more or less pacified he refused to go to bed until I did, staying closely pressed against my neck, often rubbing his head underneath my chin and letting me stroke his back as well as ruffling up his head feathers. Twice that night he woke me up with agitated grumblings, so in the end I took him into bed with me where he at last settled, nestling down on the pillow, pressed up against my neck and chin.

Before this incident I had often heard that snakes were one of the Parrot family's natural enemies, but to date I have been unable to ascertain whether or not this is really so. Certainly Solomon's attack on one does much to support this theory, as does his nervous but avid destruction of anything vaguely snake-like in character, i.e. ties, belts, string, etc. It would also explain his fright at the hose pipe, because he could conceivably have mistaken this for a snake. Also the Head Keeper at London Zoo has noticed that the parrots there generally seem ill-at-ease if children come through the houses wriggling the life-like rubber imitations about. Of course snakes love to eat eggs of many birds and maybe they do attack the smaller Parrot species, but I should have thought that macaws at any rate could dispose of one without much trouble. However, W. M. Hardy, the American ornithologist, also assumes snakes are enemies of Petz's conures. Referring to their predators at nesting time, he says: 'I assume that snakes might be successful predators on the nest contents, but probably most other potential predators, for example small mammals, would be discouraged or thwarted in attempts to enter the nest by the termite swarms that occur when the termatorium is broken open.' See Index for further reference to Petz's nests.

For a change of route to Los Angeles I went back via Yuma, which meant travelling south-west out of Phoenix, where a dam for the Salt River project was being constructed. However, except for the bridges that I crossed, there was no evidence of any river, Salt or otherwise. Without exception the river beds and arroyos were just hard, dried, cracked soil, showing no sign of ever having been a channel for gushing water. Thus the numerous 'Fishing is Forbidden from this Bridge' notices seemed amusingly incongruous.

I stayed for six weeks in Los Angeles while winding up my business affairs, selling my car and following up the requirements of Britain's Ministry of Agriculture, Fisheries and Food, for the purpose of obtaining an entry permit for Solomon. This necessitated obtaining from the official State vet: papers confirming that Solomon was in good health, and that the various States he had passed through had been free of Ornithosis during the six months preceding the date stamped on these documents.

Having duly complied with these regulations and sent the papers off to the appropriate British department, I eventually received Solomon's 'Passport', an M.A.F.F. permit allowing him to enter Britain, within a period of three months, provided he came into no contact with domestic fowl during transit, or for three months following his importation. Fortunately, since he was to be resident in a Central London flat, he would not have to be boarded in special quarantine kennels, which would have been the case had we lived on a farm.

At 10 o'clock one morning, shortly after receiving Solomon's clearance papers, we boarded the impressive Domeliner train, which was to take us via El Paso, the Colorado Rockies and over prairies to Chicago, where we changed trains for the final leg of our trip to New York. Because I wanted Solomon to travel with me rather than leave him to ride alone in the luggage car, I was required to take a first class Drawing Room. This highfalutin name seemed singularly inappropriate in referring as it did to the tiny single seat cabin, approximately three feet by six feet, that nevertheless was equipped with most essentials needed for a comfortable journey. An array of buttons produced an amazing variety of these articles, which let down from the cabin walls, or shot out from under some other fitment. They included a washbasin, a table, a footstool that converted the easy chair into a fully reclining one, a supply of iced water, and a call button for summoning the attendant porter, who would bring any other desired requirement, such as note-paper, should one wish to write in the privacy of one's cabinet rather than use the well-equipped public Reading Rooms.

A Smoking Room took care of those disappointed by the sensible ban on smoking, operative in all other public cars, while a selection of bars, buffets and dining cars supplied food and drink to suit all palates and purses. To me, as to many others, the crowning glory of this super de luxe train were the three plastic-roofed Dome cars, open to all classes, and affording glorious vistas of the swiftly-passing terrain.

A prong-horn Antelope

I spent about an hour in my cabin to get Solomon used to his surroundings before I went up to a dome car for a short visit. Once there I was fortunate enough to see a prong-horn Antelope that at first stood stiffly alert amongst some sage-brush but then made a gallant effort to race the train. Since the graceful prong-horn can run at 40 m.p.h., it kept up with us for some consider-able distance. These delightfully inquisitive antelopes have a unique danger signalling system which is part of their distinctive colouring. For when frightened the long white hair on their rump stands erect, looking like a giant powder-puff but reflecting light in the same way a mirror does. Since this is then visible for several miles, all other antelope in the vicinity can rush for cover. Having satisfied my curiosity I returned to my cabin. Although I had been away from it not in excess of fifteen minutes, and had left Solomon shut in his travel cage, he had picked the lock and was sitting on top of the luggage rack busily teasing out a knot of towelling that I had supplied for his amusement inside the cage!

Doors of the Drawing Rooms were of a plastic, concertina folding type, giving access to a narrow central corridor, allowing one to converse, in normal tones, with one's neighbour opposite. Therefore when Solomon, who had been quite silent during his first few hours on board, regaled me when I returned from the dome car with his usual piercing greeting call, he let all other occupants of the car know there was a parrot on board.

After this I had a constant stream of interested visitors and continual offers to 'baby-sit' should I be wanting to eat, or merely relax in the dome car. I was happy to take advantage of these offers, not only because they gave me greater freedom, but because I thought outside attention would help mitigate Solomon's obvious uneasiness at travelling in an 'Iron Horse'. As it happened this extra attention was of little benefit, so I kept the time I spent away from him down to a minimum. Perhaps he sensed that all was not to go smoothly on that journey.

It was therefore as well that I was with him when the mishap occurred, slight though it was. Quite suddenly a violent jerk sent small pieces of luggage and Solomon flying. Metal squealed protestingly as the great train ground to a jarring halt that again shot Solomon off balance. I expected a noisy protest from him, but there was only a quiet growl as he shivered and pressed himself close to my neck. Apparently some poor cow, having strayed on to the line, now lay squashed beneath the train.

By reason of this accident we were delayed over two hours while red-tape governing such occurrences was complied with – no easy matter since we were stranded way out on the Chihuahuan Desert. Adding discomfort to the irritation of our enforced wait was the complete breakdown of the air-conditioning system, due to the force of impact with this unfortunate beast. The lack of cool air was all the more unpleasant because we were stuck in the desert from approximately 2 p.m. to 4 p.m. when the sun's heat was truly intense. It was therefore not long before we all found ourselves the involuntary occupants of a powerful Turkish bath. In particular the dome cars became inferno-like and were soon vacated.

Eventually the porter came round with cartons of ice for first class passengers, which did help keep us cool until we were under way again. Apart, no doubt, from weight-watchers, who would find a good long sweat beneficial, the various bars most certainly prospered from the delay, their sales getting an unexpected boost from the constant demand for iced drinks.

On returning from dinner that evening I found my Drawing Room had been transformed into a bedroom. Solomon had eaten a substantial supper but remained unsettled. He did not appear to approve of the cabin's new arrangements, and even when returned to his cage and I had switched off the lights, after retiring myself, he continued to fidget and grouse. His cage was at the foot of the narrow bunk, but in the end I turned the lights on again and took Solomon out for a while to try and reassure him. This worked fine until I put him back! It seemed that if either of us was to get any sleep at all that night I would have to keep him out. As a precautionary measure against certain unavoidable accidents, I covered my arm where Solomon rested with Kleenex, and padded an area underneath it as well.

Finally we both got settled comfortably and even before I had the light out again, Solomon was sound asleep. I never sleep well in trains, but whenever I woke I found, thankfully, that Solomon was still peacefully unaware, in the land of Nod. Even a noisy scheduled stop failed to penetrate his slumbering consciousness, as did an ineffectual attempt to ease my painfully cramped arm. It was nearly 7 a.m. when he did wake and stretched his beak to its widest capacity in a mammoth yawn. He then leisurely stretched both legs and wings in turn, gave me a greeting call, flew back to his cage, and happily tucked into a large breakfast, enabling me, at long last, to massage away the numbing pins and needles from the arm he had slept on.

The journey to Chicago took two nights and one and a half days, during which time no further incidents of note occurred. Having arrived in Chicago at 9 a.m. we had the morning to fill in before leaving from another station, across town, on an overnight train to New York. Here again Solomon slept on my arm.

We arrived in New York at 9.30 a.m. and were due on board the R.M.S. Queen Mary at 3 p.m., so we had a tremendous rush around getting a final stamp required for Solomon's clearance papers at the point of departure, this time from the federal vet, picking up our tickets from Cunard's office, and finalising some business at my bank.

Much had changed in the city since I had last stayed there some four years previously. Many of its warm Brownstone buildings had given way to tall, shiny, cold, glass and metal skyscrapers, yet I was hardly able to really appreciate these changes – they merely flashed by in a confused, speedy kaleidoscope. One thing that had not changed – nor is it ever likely to – was the mad stampede which New York's pedestrian traffic and mechanised vehicles alike engage in, in travelling to their various destinations.

We soon became enmeshed in this hectic scramble, whatever our mode of transport – Shanks's pony, tram, yellow cab, or antediluvian subway. This latter belongs so much to an age long past that its frantic, cranky, jerky clattering seems to be urgently speeding one out of the twentieth century, for just one last backward glimpse, into the chapters of a history book that must soon be closed for ever.

Chapter 6

An Ocean Voyage

At last the noise and bustle of New York's dockland was behind us. Solomon's 'passport' had been examined and stamped by three Cunard officials who all made a great fuss over him. So, having been handed a receipt for his $5 ticket, off we went up the gangplank and on board R.M.S. *Queen Mary*.

A steward led the way to my cabin where shortly afterwards a young, kind, jovial butcher arrived to escort Solomon to his allotted accommodation for the voyage. A large airy 'kennel' cabin, situated next to the bridge, was set aside for furry, feathery and scaly passengers, and attached to it an enclosed 90 ft. exercise deck, solely for their benefit. On arrival there I discovered the area was barred and locked, a precautionary measure taken when the liner was in port, to prevent animals being stolen.

Solomon settled in surprisingly quickly to his quarters on the top level. His own travel cage was easily accommodated for sleeping in, while for daytime use the butcher had converted the kennel by fitting perches, feeding cups and a bath (a dog's drinking bowl being utilised for this purpose). Strangely enough, Solomon never attempted to bathe the whole time we were at sea; perhaps the sight of so much water around us was off-putting.

Already ensconced in the kennels were five dogs. Espying them, Solomon started whistling, as if calling them in – then what a commotion ensued, all the dogs barking as loud as they could with Solomon competing, until somewhere nearby a hooter went off, swiftly putting an end to noise from everyone – too much competition perhaps! Hooters went again and again. Finally they were answered by a resounding bellow from the liner's own funnels. It was the long awaited signal for three tiny tugs to manoeuvre the great ship slowly from her berth to the harbour mouth, where, under her own steam the *Queen Mary* would start her five-day ocean voyage, first to France and then to England.

When we were three miles out the kennels were unlocked, enabling owners to visit and exercise their pets, balls and other such amusements being provided by Cunard, as were bathing and grooming facilities, rugs, biscuits and the very best of food. On visiting Solomon I found two cats and a couple of alligators had joined the menagerie. Captain T. Jones was also there, making an inspection of these special passengers, and taking an interest in each. On hearing that Solomon did not usually talk he predicted that by the end of the voyage he would at least be swearing, since all parrots love to do so, thus he was sure Solomon would soon pick up this questionable accomplishment from sailors scrubbing out the exercise deck. However, I have never yet heard Solomon swear – except in his own language that is! His bride, Sheba, is nevertheless fairly proficient, so we may yet hear a duet of seamanlike oaths!

The exercise deck was certainly kept scrubbed and sparkling, much to the chagrin of a beautiful Austrian countess. She complained that her well-trained Alsatian, Rex, although a seasoned traveller (he had crossed the Atlantic seven times on various ships), respected the *Queen Mary's* spotless decks as though they were the corridor of her palace, or one of its luxurious living-rooms, and just could not, it seemed, bring himself to treat them like grassy fields, as he was supposed to. Happily a solution was soon found; a beagle and two poodles who (it was only too apparent) were not so well trained, were let out first. Sure enough they changed the hygienic quality of the deck sufficiently so as to enable Rex to obey the 'call of nature' also! This procedure, however, had to be adopted on all successive occasions.

Every afternoon at 2 p.m. the kennel hatches were closed down for an hour or so whilst Solomon was let out to fly around, as he was accustomed to doing. Meanwhile the butcher, who was clearly very fond of animals (his job as keeper and feeder of all live-stock being a volunteer one), let his various other charges out too, throwing balls for them and attending to such chores as cleaning water bowls. But apart from this time, and irrespective of any time owners spent with their pets the butcher saw to it that each animal was let out for at least five minutes in every two-and-a-half hours.

During his 'free' time Solomon paid a social call on each of his travelling companions, but none of the dogs got used to the

teasing call-in whistle that he was wont to use as his favourite piece of repertoire, at this time, whilst dive-bombing their kennels. They must all have got sore throats with barking back, yet I noticed their tails wagged hard. Rex, in particular, was singled out for this treatment, and I wondered if this was because Solomon recognised the breed as being that of one of his former companions.

Solomon's treatment of the two cats was an entirely different matter, for although they appeared to ignore him, and he'd never had any unfortunate experiences with a member of the feline family, he always gave their kennel a wide berth. On the other hand, the alligators, who also treated Solomon with disdain, were found fascinating by him. In fact, the bars of their habitat became his favourite exercise perch, for after visiting the dogs and pestering both the butcher and myself for titbits, he would swoop down on the alligators, shrieking at them with all his might, whilst hanging upside down on the bars and flapping his wings vigorously. There could be no doubt that he was egging them on, wanting some definite response to his performance. But the alligators took little notice, just occasionally one twitched a tail, yawned or rolled a heavy-lidded eyeball round, like one who is very old, viewing with great forbearance the obstreperous antics of the very young.

Actually the alligators were but two-and-a-half year olds and far from fully grown. Even so, accommodating their 2 ft. 9 in. was something of a squeeze. They had been given a double corner kennel, flanked by two radiators, and pipes ran underneath the specially fitted aluminium trough, all helping to keep their water temperature to the minimum required 70 degrees. A slight wooden ramp was also fitted in, enabling them to bask on 'dry land'.

Their owner, a professor from New York, had bought his primeval pets in Florida for $1.25 each, at a wayside fruit stall, when they were only a few inches long. As they grew he had kept them in a trough in his bathroom, not disposing of them, as many New Yorkers do, down the loo! (Hence the reputedly hazardous life of that city's sewage workers, for it is said that some of these unfortunate beasts do manage to flourish therein.)

The future home of these alligators was scheduled to be a specially converted barn at the professor's English country cottage, to which he was retiring. I have often wondered how he and they fared and whether Phil Drabble's amusingly cynical remarks about alligators as pets, in his Penguin *Book of Pets,* have as yet applied, viz.: 'The more successful you are, the more he will eat. The more he eats, the faster he'll grow and the shorter the time before you get badly bitten.'

Yet perhaps the professor relied on the fact that many reptiles, alligators included, are induced into a state of helpless submission if they are stroked gently along their belly. Well, I am by no means a sceptic and although I have never seen a demonstration of this extraordinary feat, I am quite willing to believe this is so – at a safe distance – for I can hardly claim to have been reassured by this knowledge on the various occasions I have encountered crocodiles or alligators in their natural habitat.

Anyway, my mind boggles wondering just how the professor (or anyone else) would actually manage to carry out this treatment should it prove necessary. I can well imagine him, one arm clamped firmly in his pet's jaw, while he vainly wriggles his big toe under its belly in the fervent hope that his alligator will quickly succumb to a feeling of intoxicated delight, relax its grip and roll over, the better to enjoy its owner's petting! – But rather him than me.

During our second afternoon at sea a carrier-pigeon landed with an exhausted thump on one of the decks. A member of the crew took it immediately to the officer on watch who gave it water, examined it for damage and, on finding none, removed the paper inside its ring. The butcher, having been sent for post haste, quickly prepared an upper kennel for it to rest in, adding bowls of corn, lentils and water. The pigeon drank deeply and pecked at a few lentils, only to slump amongst them in an exhausted sleep. A blanket was then hung over the kennel enabling it to rest without disturbance. Meanwhile the officer on watch checked the number taken from the bird's ring against lists he had of pigeon fanciers' clubs all over Britain, America and Europe, adding a note to say where and when the pigeon had been found. Any such birds are kept on board until they are sufficiently recovered to fly on and are then only released the next time the liner calls in at the port nearest the pigeon's home. I was told liners often get carrier pigeons coming aboard in this manner; thus, expecting them, Cunard always carry appropriate food, etc. for them.

I find it rather wonderful that this giant commercial company of the sea has the heart to find time for such thoughtful, humane actions towards creatures of a lesser order. It is, perhaps, just one reason for the happy atmosphere aboard their ships. Quite apart from human passengers, all the animals seemed content and I am sure that many of them enjoyed the trip. Solomon certainly did, revelling in the attention he received from crew and passengers, whether in or out of the kennel. In fact I cannot speak too highly of the way in which Cunard officials, as a whole, took special pride in seeing to it that pets had as pleasant a voyage as possible.

On the last night of the voyage Solomon was given a special invitation to join the Purser's cocktail party, which was hilarious as the Purser and his guests, myself included, tried to outdo each other with 'parrot' jokes that became noticeably coarser as the evening progressed, just as Solomon's behaviour became somewhat unruly. To start with he sat quietly atop his cage then, spying a piece of cheese in my hand, he flew over. In his excitement he stretched his neck forward and, being unaccustomed to alighting on bare shoulders, slipped and came to rest within the swathed décolleté of my evening dress. 'Really, my dear,' said one of the guests, 'you may be very fond of him, but must you let him get quite so familiar before dinner?' This droll remark, coupled with the surprised look on Solomon's face, caused gales of laughter from everyone!

Solomon, suddenly realising that he was the centre of attraction, deserted me, as he usually does on such occasions, and flew in turn to each of the other guests, demanding Marmite Twiglets and other like delicacies. He was obviously enjoying being able to move freely amongst people again and showed just how pleased he was by entertaining us with his call-in whistle and other party pieces. He, like everyone else, was in the traditionally gay spirits that make the really rather sad 'End of Voyage' parties such memorably bright affairs.

There was only one guest that Solomon avoided, a podgy fellow with a florid face. He was one of those boorish people who delight in teasing animals. Solomon seemed instinctively aware of this, much to 'Podgy's' annoyance. Finally, while Solomon was guzzling a titbit offered by a neighbouring guest Podgy pulled his tail. Before I had time to act Solomon flew on to his shoulder, stretched himself up, then growling, he deposited quite deliberately a large token of his disapproval! After this unseemly, if justifiable, behaviour Solomon flew to the security of my shoulder where he shrieked abuse at a spluttering Podgy, with whom, of course, he was in disgrace. Nevertheless to the rest of us Solomon's reactions seemed quite comical, causing the gathering to become almost hysterical with laughter. So I feel it was timely that a steward chanced to enter at that point announcing 'Dinner is served', and I was able to take Solomon off to my cabin, where he was being permitted to stay since it was the last night, and no more ports of call were to be made.

The steward and stewardess were happy to be left in charge whilst I went to dine. There I found the 'Bush Telegraph' had been working and news of how Solomon had had his revenge on Podgy had preceded me. The general consensus of opinion was one of approval. Thus, after dinner when I returned to my cabin, to put the finishing touches to a fancy dress hat made for one of the evening's events, I, or rather Solomon, had a constant stream of interested visitors bearing gifts of grapes, apples and nuts, and in spite of the recent titbits and late hour, he seemed pleased to be thus honoured and even ate some of the proffered fruit.

When I put on my fancy head-dress creation, entitled 'Shakespeare's Centenary', Solomon's croaky comments didn't sound too encouraging, but it did in fact win a very nice prize, much to the delight of the steward and stewardess, perhaps because they had spent part of that afternoon collecting bits and pieces for it. Eventually returning to my cabin for the night at 2.40 a.m. I found Solomon was having his own brand of fun with it, tearing Shakespeare's collar ruff (a pie-dish frill) into tiny shreds.

I had not expected to find him still awake, albeit so active, at that hour, but he greeted me quite brightly and sat happily on my shoulder, preening my hair, while I finished packing, by which time it was 3.30 a.m. He still showed little inclination for sleep so, as his cage was beside the bed, I lay back on my pillows ruffling his feathers, intending to put him to bed after five minutes or so. However, the contented rasping noises he so often makes at night sent me off to sleep instead! I awoke at 5.30 a.m. to find the light still on with Solomon gone of his own accord into his cage. He was rocking on his perch and eyeing me with a faraway expression. When I spoke to him he just made more contented noises and I wondered whether he had had any sleep at all that night.

Next morning, with the steward's help, we were almost the first off the boat and into the Customs shed where an affable Customs Officer relieved me of Solomon's clearance documents. He recognised Solomon as a conure and not a 'baby' parrot, having been to Brazil as a Merchant Marine and so been privileged to see conures and other parrots in all the glory of their freedom.

In spite of his disturbed, late night, Solomon was as friendly and good-humoured as he always is in the mornings, being quite happy to have his feathers ruffled through the bars by the officer who, with his other hand, was chalking my luggage. It was quite some time before he appeared to notice the growing queue of 'G's waiting to have their baggage cleared, and when he did he seemed in no hurry to allay their increasingly impatient sighs. It was not until he'd hailed a porter and seen my luggage loaded on to a trolley that he gave Solomon a final pat and wished him well before turning, somewhat reluctantly I thought, to the other folks waiting in his line. What a bird will do!

The train journey was an anti-climax after the lively pace of the past few days. Everyone in our compartment seemed sad at leaving the ship and their new-made friends, Solomon included. The dull, overcast day didn't help so we dozed until coffee was brought round. As it chanced the sun appeared from behind clouds at the same time and Solomon shook himself awake, gathering enough energy to greet it in particularly ear-splitting tones. I was about to apologise for him when an Australian girl passenger, who had been absent from home for over two years, burst into tears. 'I never thought I'd miss that goddam noise,' she sobbed. Apparently Solomon's raucous cries had made her feel homesick, since she had lived where flocks of small green parrots inhabited the trees. Although he refused to come out of his cage, Solomon allowed the girl to stroke his head through the bars for a short while, and for this small favour she was inordinately pleased. Soon all was quiet once more and we again nodded off.

The crowd at Victoria Station was so thick I had begun thinking I had missed my Mother when Solomon gave his special greeting call which was heard above all the hubbub and turned quite a few heads, including Mother's. It had been well over a year since he had seen her, and many miles away at that, yet spying her unexpectedly in that strange London crowd, he had

Solomon (on right) and Sheba drying off after a bath, at London Zoo

Sheba about to begin her lunch-time siesta at London Zoo

immediately recognised her. Actually I am constantly surprised at the frequency with which people ask if Solomon remembers me, should I have been absent from him for even a few days, particularly since he and his bride went to the Zoo and I now see them but once a month at the most. There are, after all, many well authenticated incidents on record indicating that parrots have exceptionally good memories, thus I had assumed this was a commonly known fact.

Following our greetings came the hoo-ha of getting luggage to the taxi rank, but that was nothing compared to the difficulty in actually obtaining a cab. The first taxi refused to take our load, the second was willing, but found it impossible to get the larger containers inside it. It seemed that no taxi had a roof rack, so despairingly, we unpacked the two largest crates.

What a performance that was, and Solomon, fed up with the long confinement in his travel cage, was straining his vocal cords to their full extent, making sure we wouldn't forget him amidst the growing pile of packaging. However, once the unpacking was complete, we at last managed to obtain not one, but two taxis, filled both to capacity and sped across London, to reach home, where a much-needed lunch was waiting.

Solomon shot out of his cage as soon as we were indoors, flying straight on to Mother's shoulder. There he stayed until lunch was over and he'd been on a tour of inspection around his new home. He then tried out various perches, but as soon as his large antique cage was assembled, the first pukka unpacking job, he sat atop that. He was evidently pleased to see it and, after considering the cage thoughtfully for a few minutes, he climbed around to examine it, both inside and out, tested all the perches, shook his head in the bath and eventually, satisfied that all was well, preened himself and settled down for a long forty winks.

Chapter 7
Merry England

In approximately 390 B.C. sacred geese, awaiting sacrifice to Minerva, gained their reputation as 'Watchdogs Extraordinary' after they had raised a midnight alarm on Capitoline Hill, thereby saving Rome from the invading Gauls and no doubt hastening their own demise as an offering of thanksgiving! Be that as it may, the use of their praiseworthy attribute has since been sadly neglected, which seems strange since many readers will know from experience just how formidable a gaggle of geese can be. A notable exception, that I recently discovered, is a gregarious flock of geese employed by Ballantine, the whisky distillers, to stand night-guard over their liquid gold usquebaugh.

I cannot presume to compare Solomon's ability with that of geese, as regards raising an alarm at the approach of midnight intruders. For one thing we were fortunate not to have any during his sojourn with us, but during the day his look-out for, and warning of 'strangers in camp' was, I am sure, as sharp and as quick off the mark as that of any self-respecting goose or gander.

This 'talent' naturally presented many problems as far as flat life, 1966, was concerned, particularly since Solomon's favourite perch was the living-room window which overlooked the square, so he was fully aware of all its comings and goings. At first his excruciatingly horrible danger screech was emitted almost unceasingly. It only needed the porter, postman, milkman, or even occupants of other flats, to turn into our block and he was in full voice. His noisy proclamations were eventually curtailed, but only after he had been formally introduced to residents and tradesmen alike. Following these elaborate ceremonies he fortunately restricted his warnings to when some hitherto unknown visitor called and to the weekly appearance of his *bête noires,* the dustmen!

Solomon, the epitome of a nosy-parker, took a great deal of interest in the activities of our neighbours. Fortunately he was soon on friendly terms with all of them and happily answered their customary 'wolf-whistles' to him as they came and went. Occasionally, if one were to hurry from the building without looking up, he would tap imperiously on a window-pane compelling them to do so.

A young baby who had arrived on the premises shortly before Solomon was put out daily, in its pram, just below our window. It soon became Solomon's self-appointed task to watch over it. During its waking hours he held the baby's interest with his antics and answered its happy gurglings with contented chuckles of his own. However, should the baby cry, or anyone other than its mother go near the pram, he began to scold until appropriate remedial action was taken. This was just one of several tasks Solomon took it upon himself to undertake, just as all our pets before him had found themselves useful chores within the family circle, an example being that of one of our Alsatians who trained herself in the art of acting as an extremely efficient 'fore-caddy', and in doing so saved us many a lost golf ball.

Taking advantage of the sunny weather when I first returned, we went on a fair number of picnics. On one such outing Solomon proved himself to be something of a cannibal. I was gnawing a thigh of chicken, at the time, while Solomon restlessly paced my shoulders getting more excited by the minute, which I thought was possibly due to the fresh country air. Suddenly, however, he grabbed the thigh bone and although staggering under the unaccustomed weight, he managed a short flight to seclusion on the car's rear seat. There he swiftly stripped the bone clean, wildly flinging the remaining flesh aside, before nibbling delicately at the gristly end. This finished, he cracked the bone itself with great dexterity and carefully picked out the marrow which he ate with evident relish.

This first bone seemed to do Solomon no harm and, in fact, over a period, it actually seemed to be of benefit, so I came to think that possibly it supplied a previous deficiency in his diet. At any rate he stopped consuming the quills of his dropped feathers, and for the first time ever, he retained the power of flight during his next full moult, which was after he'd been eating marrow from chicken bones regularly for three months or so (we normally had chicken once a week). His crippled condition during moults until then was the reason I had not released him back into one of Mexico's forests.

Actually I know of several other parrot-family members, Cockatoos in particular, who are partial to gnawing chicken bones. They too have suffered no ill effect, even after doing so for fifteen or more years. This makes me wonder whether parrots possibly devour the bones of dead birds in the wild. Perhaps some future study expedition to South America, India or Australia, will discover whether or not this is so. Certainly many grub amongst bark for insects, and Hyacinthine Macaws are known to eat small carnivores.

In fact most birds seem to be instinctively aware of what foodstuffs are beneficial to them, so as a general rule I feel pets should be allowed to select whatever they fancy. Just as when they are breeding, sick parrots may well get a craving for a particular food and eat abnormally large quantities of it. Possibly they will thus indicate a deficiency in their diet. An instance in point was Sheba's craving for grapes when she first came to us in a very sick and sorry state. Another is quoted in E. J. Boosey's book, itself referring to an item recorded in *Aviculture,* Vol. VIII, p. 53, concerning Keas bred by Mr Sydney Porter, who were already receiving an enormously varied diet. He says '. . . the parents were quite as concerned as I was, clearly indicating there was something deficient in their diet. We tried everything, even meal-worms, boiled fish, rice pudding, etc. Two young ones had already died before I thought of lettuce; when we supplied this the adults made it plain that this was what they had been waiting for. Four or five whole lettuces a day were eaten, every scrap. This nearly broke the bank, for lettuces at that time were 2/6d. each.'

Usually whenever the family sat down to eat Solomon returned to his cage where he consumed a liberal quantity of sunflower seeds before coming over to inspect our food. Being partially replete he was fussy, often becoming decidedly huffy if there was nothing he liked the look of. This occasionally meant that he would snatch the offending morsel from my mouth, fling it far across the room and, knowing that he'd be in disgrace, swiftly flit off to somewhere out of reach, vigorously wiping his beak along his chosen perch to rid from it all traces of the detested food. Alternatively he would give my cardigan a good chew, no doubt with the same purpose in view.

He was, however, always extremely gentle when taking food he did like, going to each of us in turn and giving a distinct impression of doing the person concerned a tremendous favour by thus sharing their sustenance. If guests were present Solomon invariably devoted his attentions solely to them, leaving the family strictly alone, which basic principle of psychology I have seen demonstrated by children and dogs in like circumstances. From a very early age, they all realise that visitors are far more likely to spoil them!

Fruitwise, Solomon's particular aversions were bananas and pears. A crisp, slightly tart, juicy apple remained his favourite, preferably cut close to the skin, which gave him something to scrape on (I think he liked the sound), but he also had a fancy for grapes, apricots, mangoes, papaya, including its peppery pips, peaches, dates and cooked carrot. One day I tried him with a strawberry. He did not especially care for the flesh, but he meticulously picked out and ate the miniscule pips dotting its skin, savouring each one, an operation which required infinite patience from him.

Eating strawberries, incidentally, was how Solomon accidentally got his first taste of cream and henceforth developed quite a passion for it. He soon came to recognise the sound of the egg whisk as it whipped cream up. Even on his dozy days this sound would stir him into action. Almost immediately he would appear in the kitchen, shrieking excitedly, as he flew back and forth from door to shoulder of whosoever was cooking, giving their cheeks impatient dabs until he'd received his portion. He then made such a delightful, almost purring noise as he lapped the cream it was hard to resist the temptation to give him more, as for obvious reasons his helping was always tiny.

Solomon was by no means a greedy bird and I never knew him to steal, so we could leave him alone for some considerable time with a bowl full of cream, and in spite of his passion for it he never made any attempt to help himself. In any case, being a sociable little fellow, he much preferred eating *en famille*. Thus on the odd occasions when we were out without him, we found that even his sunflower seeds had remained untouched, something he would immediately rectify, after greetings, on our return. Oddly enough, I have never heard of any tame, pet parrot stealing. Having observed their eating habits in natural surroundings it is something I would have expected them to do, but all my parrot-owning friends report them to be thoroughly reliable in this respect. Maybe this is partially due to their need and craving for attention from their human companions.

The only non-food that Solomon enjoyed was Yardley's

Solomon with Jimmy

lipstick. He seemed, as I do, to like its rosewater flavour, or perhaps its creamy consistency, because whenever he noticed me applying any, he would fly over to have a dig at the tube, or if that course was denied him he invariably attempted to lick the stuff off my lips. Yet on the odd occasions when I used another brand he took no notice of it.

The Christmas holidays meant that my young nephews, Jimmy and Ian, were able to become acquainted with Solomon, who at first displayed his usual caution when confronted with children, but he did not remain aloof for long, particularly when Jimmy and Ian began vying for his favour by plying him with his favourite Royal Hawaiian Macadamia nuts and their Brazilian rival. Therefore in a remarkably short space of time he was taking it in turns to be given rides on their shoulders, and sometimes even on their heads!

All animals are at times perverse in ignoring those humans who seek to be friendly, whilst pestering those who would rather do without their attentions. So it was with Solomon and my

Solomon taking a ride on Ian's head

brother, John. Normally Solomon was not wont to seek out voluntarily the company of any male, unless some enticement was offered; even then he viewed their presence with caution. Nevertheless he soon made John the exception to this rule of his – an exception which provided Jimmy and Ian especially with a great deal of amusement; so much so that Solomon was very often quietly incited by the boys to pursue their father and even, on occasion, egged on by me.

Actually John rather admired our feathered friend, but preferred him at a distance, for he did not particularly appreciate his ears being nibbled – sign of affection though it was. Nor, for that matter, did he relish being 'fanned' at close quarters on those icy mornings. Therefore he tended to duck out of Solomon's flight path. Not unnaturally this had the effect of strengthening Solomon's desire to perch upon his broad shoulders and there inevitably followed a hilarious, noisy chase around the flat, Solomon's hot pursuit of John being closely followed by Jimmy and Ian shouting wild encouragements. Since Solomon did not always achieve his goal he began to use cunning, waiting to catch John unawares, such as when he was engrossed with the morning newspaper, or more often than not, when he was using the telephone. Once installed, no amount of physical jerks on John's part could shake him off – 'No' always was his favourite word!

There were other occasions when Solomon was perverse. For instance, he occasionally refused when I wanted him to come off a particular perch – perhaps because he did not like the look of what I had in mind for him to do. However, if my entreaties failed and I pretended to ignore him for a while, he would very soon come to me of his own accord. His independence had thus been established, or, as the Chinese would put it, 'his face had been saved'. Yet possibly one of the most endearing traits of Solomon's character is his manner of acknowledging one whenever one speaks directly to him. Sometimes his response is coy, at other times all too lively, and when he can think of none other, he'll stretch a wing or give a contented waggle of his tail.

We spent Christmas itself at the riverside home of our Auntie Betty. Solomon always loved his days at Wraysbury, so was as pleased as the rest of us to be there at this time. For one thing, in warm weather, he had enjoyed the freedom of her garden with its gnarled old apple tree, quite apart from his keen interest in activity on the river, and that closer to hand, since here too he enjoyed the lavish attention of my young cousin, Sarah, and the company of Chippy, her budgerigar.

For some months Solomon had quite clearly missed a safe spot where he could sit freely out in the trees. Even in warm weather we had had to curtail this in inner London, mainly because of the vast numbers of predatory cats living in our square. I think he also missed frequent outings in the car, as I did, but this was an unavoidable cut, because for the first eighteen months after returning to England, I worked in the exhibition department of a large London store, whilst building up my free-lance contacts. The nature of this work inevitably meant that the majority of my weekends were fully occupied at the store, leaving no time for countryside jaunts. It also meant that I saw very little of Solomon during this time. Naturally his presence would not have been very welcome at the store since, even I have to admit, his endearing enthusiasm for assisting me in my projects was usually more of a hindrance than a help.

At any rate frustration at lack of outings, combined with the other factors mentioned had, that Christmas, culminated in bringing out in Solomon his breed's propensity for self-disfiguration, by way of plucking out bosom feathers and those around his back. This was rather annoying, particularly as we were in full agreement with W. T. Greene's charmingly phrased sentiments: 'We have advised the placing of soft pieces of wood in the cages, so that the birds may exercise their beaks in a more congenial manner than on their own plumage.' Because we agreed (though not with the caged bit) we acknowledged and pandered to Solomon's need/right to gnaw and thereby rapidly demolish a particular cupboard door. Here he, and later Sheba also, spent up to ten minutes each day 'honing' their beaks. He clearly considered it part of his own special territory within the flat, and after all he did oblige us by confining this activity to one door only!

However, our solicitude had, for some weeks before Christmas, been of no avail. To quote the wise Duke of Bedford: 'No parrakeet in existence is more addicted to the vice of feather plucking; only the plainest diet combined with plenty of exercise in a large outdoor aviary and a companion of the opposite sex will prevent some birds disfiguring themselves. The absence of any one of these factors will at once cause them to begin.'

The result of Solomon's self-inflicted torture was an appearance so disreputable it caused my cousin Joan succinctly to pronounce him 'oven-ready'! And indeed, on comparing Solomon's bosom with that of the plump, stuffed turkey awaiting its roasting, I could truly see little difference.

Actually, from his choice of perch, one got the impression he was quite willing to share the turkey's fate. The day was bitterly cold and perhaps the falling snow reminded him of Chicago, for having made his usual tour of inspection on arrival at Aunt Betty's, he shunned the normally popular window perches, choosing instead to settle on the Aga's plate rack. It was not the healthiest, nor the safest place for him, but it was unquestionably the warmest, and fortunately for him my aunt was unperturbed by his presence there. He was certainly no trouble, the steamy heat making him drowsy, content and therefore amenable. Even the newspaper spread as a precaution underneath him was unnecessary, for he considerately made the requisite number of sorties back to his cage when acknowledging the call of nature.

The following Easter my mother and I decided to visit Malta, my brother being stationed there at the time. We were to be away several weeks and because Solomon was always so happy at Wraysbury, we gladly took advantage of Joan's offer to look after him during our stay. Accordingly, a few days before we went, Solomon, with large cage, was duly installed beside his friend Chippy, in the wide bay window of Joan's living-room where he enjoyed panoramic views of the river Thames and its interesting attendant activities.

We spent the day there which, as usual, was wholly enjoyed by all of us, except for a short row on the river that Solomon alone did not appreciate being, as he was, nervous when at close quarters with swans and ducks, to say nothing of our dinghy's oars. Although I knew Solomon would be perfectly happy and well-looked after, the moment of departure was poignant, because I had never before left him for any length of time, and Solomon sensing this was loathe to leave my shoulder, which made it all the worse when the time came to take our leave. However, by the next day he apparently showed no signs of missing me, obviously being well satisfied with the attention given to him by Sarah, who had been detailed not only to cosset him, but clear up the gargantuan mess he created daily!

When we returned from Malta and subsequently went to fetch Solomon, we found him decidedly reluctant to end his riverside holiday, which apparently he had enjoyed immensely. Aunt Betty, Joan and Sarah all confirmed that 'Dirty Dick', as by then he had been aptly nicknamed, had made himself very much at home there, so much so that he had even thrown a tantrum, when one morning, he was unable to have Joan's undivided attention. This was because Joan had friends in for coffee and had prevented him from joining their party on the verandah. When Solomon found his shrieks of protest were not getting the desired reaction, he characteristically obtained his vengeance by having a good chew at one of the hall curtains. By the time Joan became aware of his ominous silence and looked for its cause, Solomon had already managed to give the curtain in question the appearance of Gruyere cheese!

For a few days after his return to the flat Solomon's chattering consisted mainly of a repetitive mimicry of Chippy's repertoire, but having worked this out of his system, we never again heard him utter any part of it. Nevertheless Solomon continued to increase his own vocabulary of strange noises, being greatly assisted in this by B.B.C.'s 'sound archives'. His favourite programme on radio was 'Wild Bird Recordings', presented by Ludwig Koch and his wife Elsie. He often became very excited and sometimes answered the calls of the birds. Should they be danger cries he would occasionally fly wildly about the room and it then took considerable patience to steady him down again.

Solomon also enjoyed a good thriller, with all its attendant spine-chilling music, owl hoots, squealing tyres and so forth, plus the inevitable creepy creaking of a slowly opening door or chest. This latter sound in particular intrigued him, and he soon became far too proficient at it for my peace of mind, especially since he had a pronounced inclination to play practical jokes, so having perfected his imitation of a creaking door he often made one think that a third party had entered the flat. This was especially effective because he usually waited to perform when he was on his own in a room, and often preceded it by knocking loudly on something wooden. We were tricked many times by Solomon's use of this noise, which gave him ample opportunity to indulge in yet another favourite – his gleeful, witchy cackle – which would follow us down the passage as we went to the front door! Another clever imitation, less wearing on the carpets, was his copy of blackbird calls, possibly picked up from a semi-tame member of the species, which comes regularly to our window-sill for food.

Solomon's temperament was always greatly affected by the weather. On rainy days he would stare pensively out of the window. It seemed he gazed past the bleak scene and saw instead the beloved rain forest of his birth. At these times he looked so woe-begone that he filled one with pity for him. If he had ever flown off for good I think it would have been then, but as it was whenever he did go out in the rain, and he loved to do so, he very soon became so waterlogged he was unable to sustain his flights. On sunny days, however, he was cheerful, noisy and invariably looked for some mischief to get up to around the house, rather than outside.

In winter Solomon sensibly spent the greater part of any day in a state of hibernation in the kitchen, while during the evening he, like the rest of us, appreciated the warmth of blazing pine logs, or a large coal fire. Thus he would sit for hours on the knee or foot of whosoever was closest to this oldest of man's domestic comforts. Occasionally he took a keen interest in some television programme, but it never seemed to give him the same enjoyment as radio did, and generally the goggle-box bored him. When it did, he would rub his head along my knee, in a thoroughly soppy manner and, nestling down on my lap, he'd quietly invite me to ruffle his head feathers. Sometimes it had a completely relaxing effect on him and he kept me at it for hours; at other times, feeling more lively, he would give my finger playful nips or pick purls of wool from my cardigan even as I ruffled his feathers.

Before settling down for the evening he often attended to important personal chores, such as giving himself a pedicure, which he often followed up by giving me a manicure, diligently poking his beak gently under my finger nails to remove any foreign bodies. This done, he nibbled at any split nails 'til they were more to his satisfaction, and finished off by tidying up any rough skin round about. Although he was normally gentle and did a good job, he occasionally lost patience and yanked painfully at an offending piece of jagged cuticle thereby aggravating its condition.

One evening my brother, who had returned to London for a conference, was sitting legs crossed, on the opposite side of the fire from me, engrossed in *The Times,* while Solomon sat on my trousered-knee, steadily denuding the corduroy of its pile. He had for some time though been regarding John's foot with interest. There was a wicked gleam in his eye as eventually he scurried quietly down my leg and stepped, ever so softly, on to John's shoe. Once there he began, quite deliberately, to untie the shoe-lace. Needless to say his mischief did not go undetected for long. *The Times* wasn't that powerful an analgesic, besides Solomon had quickly become excited when he began his tug-of-war with the shoelace, while Mother and I would anyway have given the show away completely by laughing.

In summer Solomon was an extremely early riser, but not so on cold, dark, winter mornings, when he stayed abed until breakfast was well under way and he'd had his shivery bite – a pellet of butter and breadcrumbs. Perversely, on the occasional Sunday when the family decided to lie in, Solomon got fed up waiting for us to come through and as in summer he would flit into my bedroom, perch on the dressing-table mirror and regale his image with cheery greetings, taking not the slightest notice of any odd socks thrown vaguely in his direction. If he had not managed to stir us with his rally call, as piercing as any army bugle, he began dive-bombing the beds, until in the end we just had to get up.

If we then took breakfast back to bed he subscribed to the principle 'If you can't beat them, join them', and perched on the edge of the tray to do just that. First he would come to me for hot, buttered toast and then join my mother for a 'cuppa' which, considering his usual intake of liquid, was quite liberal, and taken from a saucer. Having had his fill he himself would then retire for a comfortable forty winks amongst my blankets.

Come the summer, I made several trips to Wiltshire, where Jimmy and Ian were at school. I stayed with some particularly dear friends, Carolyn and Ronald Stevenson, and their four delightful children, Louisa, James, Shannon and baby Henrietta, who first met Solomon one evening, when of course he was sleepy and therefore grumpily anti-social. But Louisa, James and

Shannon were not in the least put off by that; after all it was almost their bedtime too and they still felt lively!

Actually Solomon had already met Carolyn at our flat and he'd taken an instant liking to her, settling happily on her shoulder even before any introductions had been made, which was indeed a precedent, so possibly her presence with the children reassured him. At any rate, in spite of the late hour, he gave in gracefully to their earnest attentions and was not the least frightened by boisterous high spirits. Normally possessive over his seed dishes, he turned a blind eye when little hands stretched inside his cage, and offered him the contents to break the ice! He had already eaten well on the way down in the car, but accepted all that the children pressed on him. Later, when Louisa, James and Shannon, having had their baths, returned downstairs for supper and a story Solomon even found room for a sampling of their biscuits. After which, being thoroughly replete, he made himself at home by going to roost on one of the pictures, gracing the living-room walls, knocking three askew before finding one to his liking.

It was about this time that I began a concentrated effort to find Solomon a mate and we visited many bird farms and sanctuaries in the hope of doing so, but no one had even a closely related species. In the end I tried London Zoo. They too had no other Petz's Conure, but the Curator of Birds was keen to have Solomon anyway, saying he would make every effort to obtain a mate for him. Initially I was not at all taken with this idea. Apart from anything else I loathe to see caged animals of any sort. Also the parrot house, at that time, used such fearfully small and inadequate housing for their inmates, I knew that Solomon, never having been closely confined, would in the circumstances be utterly miserable. However, new indoor cages, not ideal, but allowing room for short flights, were being constructed, while birds in breeding aviaries are able to approach as natural a way of life as is possible for the majority of caged birds, although when funds become available, these too have room for improvement.

The Curator himself has an extremely humanitarian outlook in regard to the mental, as well as the physical, wellbeing of his charges. Consequently he really does do his utmost to pair all of them, one reason being that he is particularly keen to see the Zoo become established as a breeding ground for parrots. So he promised he would make every effort to obtain a mate for Solomon, should I give him to the zoo.

I too dislike keeping any animal, including the domesticated dog, without a companion of its ilk, believing that generally speaking, however genuinely fond an animal is of human company, there are bound to be times when it misses the presence of its own kind. Thus, much as I would love to be surrounded by animals of many kinds, including water-babies such as seals and dolphins, I resist the temptation to accept or keep any, since quite obviously I would not be able to provide them with my idea of their necessary freedom in a small London flat, where at times I feel all too restricted myself.

Thus the more I thought about Solomon living at the Zoo, particularly if he were housed in an outdoor aviary, the more the idea appealed to me, so I finally agreed to it, provided he had a companion, and also that he did not show any signs of pining. But it was indeed a very difficult decision to make. Meanwhile I thought it best to keep Solomon with me until remodelling improvements at the parrot house were complete, by which time both the Curator and I hoped he would have a girl friend.

That particular summer seemed to pass very quickly, possibly because I had given up work at the store, having several free-lance commissions in hand. One of them was converting a disused basement into a Buttery for the girls at a secretarial school in Knightsbridge, run by Lucie Clayton Ltd who are perhaps better known for their 'Model' Girl Agency. My work here was tremendous fun, since the owners, Evelyn and Leslie Kark, were 'model' clients, also the job was a challenge, and it was grand to be free-lance again.

On two weekend occasions when I went to the school to work on some murals, I took Solomon with me, which as usual, he seemed to enjoy, although the second of these visits was a near-disaster for him. I had almost finished spraying in some clouds when Solomon decided to inspect the arcadian landscape. Unfortunately his chosen flight path crossed that of the Crown emulsion being sprayed, and swift though his passage was, my shimmering green pet emerged an albino!

Quick action with hot water was needed to remove the emulsion. None being available on the premises at that time, I gave him a ducking under the cold-water tap to keep the paint wet and dashed next door to the Norway Food Centre's loo where, much to the amused sympathy of the staff, he had his first and last hot-water bath. I can't pretend it was enjoyed, but at least the paint came off, all but on one tail feather. That remained to 'tell the tale' until his next full moult!

Chapter 8
Sheba at Last

Having finished our shopping at Harrods one Saturday morning we visited their Pet Department, which that day was perhaps better described as a miniature zoo. Apart from various members of the psittacidae family and the normal selection of domestic pets, there were bush-babies, snakes, mongooses, monkeys and even a fully-fledged ant-eater. In spite of all these interesting distractions I was quick to spot a shabby Petz's conure huddled miserably on a high-up branch, in a mixed aviary of other small birds like cockatiels.

Shabby or not, the conure 'looked' female, so it seemed that at long last we had found a possible mate for Solomon; an exciting moment. Excitement that soon meant spending the weekend on tenterhooks as Harrods was closing, so there was insufficient time for a close inspection of the conure, let alone arranging for its purchase. Anyway the poor thing looked so ill I did wonder if it would survive the weekend.

A 'phone call first thing on Monday morning ascertained that it had. So this was quickly followed with a call to the Curator at London Zoo to establish whether or not the Zoo would be interested, and if so, to ask them to make arrangements to vet the conure regarding its health, and as far as possible to determine its sex.

I spent many anxious hours waiting for the Curator's return call, but when it did come through I was delighted to learn that the Zoo was indeed willing to purchase the conure as a mate for Solomon, but due to the fearful neglect that the poor creature was suffering from, he felt it would be far better if the two made their acquaintance in the flat. This was mainly so that she could have the extra cosseting that would get her back to full health. Naturally I was very happy that this should be so and was only disappointed that it was too late for me to pick the bird up that very day.

I was also unable to collect her the next day since at the time I was engaged on the design of 'A Careers Promotion Caravan' for the National Dairy Council. Its first appearance was to be at Olympia's Royal Dairy Show, and because of meeting exhibition deadlines, work on it couldn't be delayed. So it was not until Wednesday afternoon that I again visited Harrods, taking Solomon's travel cage with me.

The conure protested volubly as she was netted and caged. The assistant then disappeared with her into a back room and was away a long time. I was horrified on his return to see the cage enmeshed with string. His uncalled for handiwork had terrified Sheba, as the conure came to be called. Upset as I was, there was little point in protesting for the damage had already been done. Anyway I realised that the assistant really had thought he was being helpful in ensuring that Sheba would not escape through the bars that Solomon had long since snapped off in the Colorado Desert.

The best thing was to get her home as quickly as possible before attempting to undo the spaghetti-like maze that had possibly made Sheba feel she was surrounded by snakes. Luckily the doorman was keeping an eye on my car at a side entrance, so we were soon on our way.

I spoke softly to the conure but there was no response until I strung together a few remembered words of Spanish. '*Lorita* (the South American name for pet parrots), *amigo, masha, mañana, la jolla, lorita.*' They certainly made no sense except that the sounds were right and Sheba looked at me, an expression of curious interest in her enormous, pretty eyes. At that point there was little else about her that was attractive. She really was greatly neglected. One nostril was torn and oozing putrid matter, while her feathers were so fouled that the car soon began to smell like a filthy henhouse. Subsequently I discovered her to be suffering from enteritis and this is no doubt what was causing the terrible stench.

Since for a few moments my attention had been directed more towards Sheba than the road I had of necessity to brake in a harsher manner than usual. Even so, I was startled to hear her thud to the cage floor. I pulled in while she struggled back on to a perch. It was then, with a pitying wave of nausea, that I realised why she had lost her balance. She had no claws with which to cling – instead her tarsi ended in gorey sores. I just cannot imagine why I'd previously been unaware of this torturous maiming; it was then all too obvious. I drove with particular care after this, but even so Sheba had to hold tight with her beak to keep balanced on the perch.

The conure's favourable reaction to Spanish sounds made me wonder if she had been brought but recently from Mexico. I made several unsuccessful attempts to find out something of Sheba's past history, feeling it would have been an important aid in knowing how best to coax away her fears, but the most I learnt was that Harrods had bought her from a man whose wife had died and he was unwilling to take care of her. Thus one can merely guesss how she came to lose her claws; perhaps they were caught in a door being slammed. However this tragedy happened I personally think she also suffered ill-treatment at the hands of some vile sadist, because even months of sheer neglect could hardly have caused her agonising fear of the human race, which was much, much more severe than that of wild birds.

I was also unable to learn Sheba's original name. It seems an unnecessary, if minor, cruelty to deprive second-hand pets of their name, yet this omission is common amongst pet shop dealers, and even applies to canines. At any rate I tried the new conure with many, but none seemed to ring a bell with her, so Sheba she became and, pronounced with a Spanish accent, she very soon responded to it.

The first evening Sheba spent in the flat was not a happy one for her. She was too distressed by the move, the tiny strung-up cage (which filled her with more terror as I removed the string) and the strange surroundings, even to bother with eating, so I wondered whether I would have a similar ordeal to the one I had at first with Solomon. I had hoped that Solomon's presence would reassure her, but it did not. The two conures seemed studiedly to ignore each other. In the end, I covered all but the front of Sheba's cage, put it in a warm spot in view of Solomon and left her in peace.

Next morning the sun was shining and Sheba, hearing Solomon crack his seeds, started on hers. We put her, still caged, by an open window and Solomon suddenly showed an interest in her presence. He flew across to her cage, quizzed Sheba for a few minutes then, leaning in through the broken bars, he acted in a most ungentlemanly way. Unlike me, having been quick to see the injury to Sheba's feet, he immediately made a deliberate attempt to bite them.

He got severely ticked-off by both Mother and me, but was not in the least contrite, and since I had prevented him from mauling Sheba he turned on me instead! Sheba had uttered but one faint squeal and sat still, looking extremely unhappy. Sheba was very gentle but at that time she was probably far too weak to retaliate, even had she wanted to, as she was suffering from sore eyes and Rhinitis as well as enteritis. The balance between health and death is especially delicate in birds, possibly because they cannot for long store nutritional benefits from their food. Fortunately Sheba made a steady recovery.

In spite of looking thoroughly miserable for the rest of the day, Sheba ate continuously, which was, of course, a good sign. We offered her apple but she found it difficult to hold, and in the end gave up the unequal struggle. But when Mother handed her a grape Sheba got so excited she even made a tentative move to take it from her fingers. The grape was savoured until every last drop of juice, flesh and skin had been consumed. Thus she avidly devoured all grapes subsequently given to her. Since they are so full of glucose it was probably grapes that gave her the energy to recover; during that first week she ate about fifteen a day, a lot for so small a bird.

Between making a tremendous fuss over both Mother and myself, Solomon showed a distressing inclination to repeat his morning attack on Sheba. I was at a loss to know why he should do this when on previous encounters with other birds he had been extremely friendly towards them. It certainly was not from jealousy as regards my attention to the newcomer, for various abandoned fledgings and an injured sparrow had had a temporary home in the travel cage and had had a great deal of attention from me. In fact he had been slightly nervous of the sparrow when it first made its appearance, but at no time had he attacked any of these strangers. It could be that his assault on Sheba was a deep-rooted instinct, which many wild birds have, for 'humanely' destroying their injured and deformed congeners. Yet I have often wondered whether this applies to parrots, having read several truly heart-rending accounts where the surviving member of a devoted 'tame' pair has made desperate efforts to try and revive its dead partner.

Perhaps deep down Solomon knew that this particular 'Lady in Distress' was no mere visitor and was eventually to disrupt his established mode of life. Or, alternatively, his aggression may have been a prelude to his love-play. Many animals, humans included, as immortalised in Noel Coward's *Private Lives*, enjoy a good tiff before getting 'goofy' over each other, and Solomon often gave me a few sharp nips, as a preliminary to fanning out his neck feathers and inviting me to caress him there. Whatever the reason for Solomon's disgraceful behaviour it was hardly a fortuitous start to their relationship, and was particularly distressing in view of Sheba's previous and obviously unhappy experience.

On Sheba's second evening in the flat we shut Solomon in his cage and opened the little one up. Although Sheba had not attempted to leave her cramped quarters through the broken bars, she needed no encouragement to leave through its doorway. Having stretched her wings she made straight for Solomon's cage, where of course, her feet were an easy target for his savage beak. Once again Sheba made no effort to retaliate, or move away. In the end I pulled Solomon off while Mother got a bemused Sheba back into the travel cage, at which she protested volubly. Solomon was as annoyed with me as I was with him, and he sulked for the rest of the evening, turning his back when I spoke to him.

Next day Sheba had a longer outing, but fared little better as regards treatment from Solomon. My Mother, having found him eating in his cage soon after breakfast, had shut him in and let Sheba out. Again the silly creature made a bee-line for his cage. Although she landed on its top branch she soon hopped down within striking distance of Solomon's beak, but finally, having been knocked to the floor she sensibly flew off to sit in the sun at the window.

Meanwhile Solomon worked at the catch on his cage door. Eventually getting it open he flew to Sheba, picked a fight and knocked her to the floor once more. After this Solomon was removed to the kitchen. Since Sheba was too frightened to come to hand, Mother offered her the end of a broomstick. This mode of transport Sheba accepted and was given a dignified ride back to the window-sill where she was left in peace for a few hours.

By late afternoon we discovered she had found her way into Solomon's cage and was happily tucking into his seeds. Having had her fill, she settled herself amongst the remainder and we hadn't the heart to disturb her. Of course this posed a great many problems. Apart from feeling that Solomon would go beserk if he found her there, I was very afraid he would catch her infections. On the other hand Solomon was far from being such a creature of habit as to be disturbed by a change of routine, so I decided to hand feed him and let him roost on my arm, as he had done in the 'domeliner'.

Actually it was late in the evening when Solomon noticed Sheba's whereabouts. Luckily she had by then moved over to the soft Balsa wood perch running alongside his bath. It was also fortunate that we had taken the precaution of disinfecting seed cups etc. when she had moved, for as soon as Solomon saw her he shot from my lap, where he had been having his feathers ruffled and, without warning, made a bee-line for his bed perch. Once there he surprised us by giving Sheba a modest greeting, even bowing to her a few times. He, it seemed, was not in the least put out to find Sheba as his bedfellow. We stayed up later than usual to ascertain that all would remain peaceable, which to our surprised relief it did.

5.30 a.m. and the anticipated explosion occurred. Solomon had felled Sheba to the cage floor and had just dropped on top of her when I entered. Sheba looked dazed; perhaps she was still half asleep, as I was. I picked Solomon up bodily as he was still too full of fury at his girl-friend to object to being handled in this perfunctory way. I then took him through to the bedroom, shut the cage door on Sheba, and made an early morning cuppa. This done, I checked in on her and found her nestled down amongst Solomon's seeds again. As to that particular brute, he grumbled steadily for over an hour.

We decided to forgo our usual weekend trip to the country – taking two 'Green Devils' would pose far too many problems. Anyway I doubted that Sheba was in a fit state to travel. Since, however, the day was warm and sunny we decided to risk giving her a much needed bath. I cannot say she enjoyed this, but she did not seem too frightened, and once she had had a good soak we let her out for the final spray. She began to fluff her feathers then and looked slightly less miserable; probably she had begun to realise that we wished her no harm. Nevertheless she still would not come to hand, even though tempted with a grape; but once again she clambered quite happily on to a broomstick and was thus carried back to the living-room.

Meanwhile we encouraged Solomon to bathe, helping him to become waterlogged in the hope that it would prevent further squabbles, which it did. Both did justice to their 'shivery' bites of granola biscuit, apple and grapes.

The flat edge of the sash-window cross-bar made an ideal surface for Sheba to eat on because, since she had no claws, she had difficulty in foot-holding her food in the normal parrot fashion, so she was able to use the cross-bar as a third hand, flattening herself out and resting her food against it. Since it was so much easier for her we always let her eat there, and of course Solomon followed suit.

As they dried, Solomon and Sheba made gradual moves towards the centre of the window, where we had deposited a huge pile of sunflower seeds to act as a barrier between them. Sheba, looking and smelling more socially acceptable, was the first to take a tentative peck at one. But Solomon was quick to follow suit and there followed a contest that seemed designed to find the champion sunflower-seed eater in the world, in the shortest time possible.

The sound of cracking seeds went on for hours and the mess the two of them made was Augean. In spite of Sheba's seemingly insatiable appetite Solomon eventually won the contest hands down. His ego may have been inflated, but so was his 'tum', and I imagine his interior felt quite uncomfortable for some considerable time afterwards for he had eaten so much that the consequentially abnormally large bulge of his crop made its covering feathers stick straight out in a truly comical fashion. The one good side-effect being that he was so satiated he was quite unable to move, sitting with legs straddled wide, and thereby assuring, if accidentally, that Sheba was unharassed for the remainder of that day.

As evening drew nigh Sheba again scorned the travel cage, flying instead to Solomon's and taking up residence, as on the previous evening, beside his bath. Since Sheba thereby made it quite clear that she intended co-habiting with Solomon whatever his feelings were on the subject, I exchanged the bath for her own containers of seeds and water, taking it as an encouraging sign that she stayed put when I did so. Her long day had made her tired and she was yawning her head off soon after 6 p.m. Somehow this action always looks so comical when performed by a bird.

Solomon also chose to have an early night and in spite of his bullying, Sheba must have felt some sort of confidence from having him close, because as soon as her espoused entered the cage she tucked her head under her wing and went soundly off to sleep. As on the previous evening Solomon ignored his zealous girl-friend, but as if he hadn't had enough, stretched over awkwardly to sample a few of her seeds.

So was begun a strange routine, the two conures peaceably sharing their sleeping quarters, while causing havoc in the flat during the day. Apart from their squabbling, Sheba was by no means 'house-trained' and although of nervous disposition, she was extremely curious about her surroundings, so we began to find her 'calling cards' in every room. Apart from this Sheba had obviously made up her mind that Solomon was her ideal mate, in spite of his aggression towards her. Consequently she chased him from room to room and perch to perch. This was an exhausting business, especially for my Mother who was in during the day, because although Solomon maintained an uneasy truce with Sheba when someone was in the room, he would quickly go into the attack if we did not keep an eye on him.

Thus for Sheba the course of true love certainly did not run smooth. But undiscouraged she kept up her pursuit, and being a really strong flier and amply possessed of feminine charm and wiles, she generally became quite adept at avoiding Solomon's attacks. Yet even when she did not, she still made no effort to fight back.

What it was that eventually provoked our normally gentle Sheba sufficiently to retaliate we have no idea, as no one was in the room with them at the time their Knock-out bout started. They had, as usual, been 'sparring' verbally for quite some time, when we became aware of heavily beating wings and angry squawks. Our entry was met with flurrying feathers, but it momentarily disrupted their battle royal, which was subsequently disastrous. Each having taken a reconnaissance flight, they collided with such force that Sheba was flung into the bookcase, while Solomon, hitting one of the living-room walls, rebounded and crashed into the kitchen window.

Both, we found, were unconscious, Solomon behind the 'fridge, and Sheba amongst the books. I was almost hysterical, feeling they had killed each other. The throbbing palpitations of their hearts were hardly reassuring since their eyes were glazed. For an hour we nursed them. They appeared to be in a state of shock, because in spite of being cupped in our hands, their feet and beaks remained icy. Sheba was the first to show signs of life and when she began to stir Mother put her into the partially covered cage and set a dimplex heater in front of it for comforting warmth. There she nestled down in a seed dish. Solomon, being tamer, was cosseted until he was well able to stand on his feet, but he too seemed glad to recover quietly in his cage. In fact both birds stayed there for the remainder of the day, almost without stirring.

Naturally I was extremely upset by the turn of events, despairing that they would ever become compatible. However, the Curator at London Zoo felt that three weeks was early days for a lasting friendship to have formed. I am glad to say his judgment was, of course, perfectly correct. Looking at them now it is really hard to believe that they were ever indifferent to each other's charms, but in fact, this major clash was the turning point in their relationship and they were none the worse for it, apart from having temporarily bruised beaks, and being the lighter for a few missing feathers!

The transformation did not come overnight, but Solomon was now definitely half-hearted in his attempts to chivvy Sheba. He still made a terrific fuss over Mother and myself but he was not nearly so single-minded about it, and it only needed Sheba to call from another room and he was off to see just what she was up to.

Sheba, her health now rapidly improving, soon turned out to be quite a coquette, prettily encouraging Solomon to her side – once she was at a safe distance from him! She also began to take food from Mother's fingers and welcome her with a greeting call such as Solomon used for me, and like Solomon, who knew the sound of the car engine, or the approach of my footsteps before I was in sight, she would get duly excited by Mother's approach. But for some reason she remained much more nervous of me than she did of Mother. Thus she never flew down the passage to greet me, as Solomon did as soon as he heard my key turn in the lock.

The two conures spent most of the daylight hours at the living-room window. Every morning we wedged a cream pot at its centre, in an effort to keep them apart, yet both worked ener-getically until they had not only dislodged, but discarded it. They then began manoeuvres that were both comical but tiring to watch as they continued throughout the day. Having removed the cream pot, they would retire to corners of the window furthest away from each other. Then Solomon, in response to Sheba's blatant encouragements, would slowly sidle up to her. Sheba, appearing heedless of his tactics, would wait until his beak was within striking range, at which point she gave an elegant stretch of her wings and, fluttering over Solomon's back, she landed at a safe distance from him on the far side, and thus she con-tinued to outwit him in a supremely ladylike manner. Eventually though, they would sit quite close together, looking with such *affectuoso* at each other, that it was not long before our neighbours began referring to them as 'the goofy two'.

In spite of their truce the flat was hardly peaceful, for the friendlier that Solomon and Sheba got the noisier they became. Their racket having one day reached unbearably irritating pro-portions, and mild admonishments having failed to quieten them, my Mother told them quite forcibly to 'shut up', whereupon Sheba, with amazing alacrity and equal force, turned round re-torting: 'You shut up!' She shocked Solomon at least into silence, but had Mother and myself laughing. This is, of course, a marvellous example of the terrific sense of humorous timing that many parrots possess.

As with Solomon, there was nothing 'parrot-like' about Sheba's behaviour, so the two together proved quite a handful as we never knew what mischief they would get up to next. And, al-though Sheba was far gentler natured than Solomon, it was always she who egged him on to some new adventure, but luckily he hardly shared her interest in the contents of cupboard or drawers. Once Sheba nestled down for several hours amongst some precious cashmere sweaters and showed distinct reluctance to leave, even after due encouragement from Solomon, which I took as a hopeful sign that she was wanting to raise a family. Another time we accidentally shut her in the wardrobe and it was only her squawks of protest which made us aware of her presence therein.

Because of her insatiable curiosity, we were not surprised when interrupted in doling out seeds one day, to find on our return Sheba's tail emerging from a half-filled jar of hemp-seeds. She was balanced precariously on the rim, head down, clouding the inside of the jar, but she righted herself in due course and flew off triumphantly with one of the tiny seeds. Solomon, not to be outdone, followed suit and thus, in this ridiculous manner, they thereafter took their daily ration of cannabis.

The one thing we could depend upon Solomon and Sheba to do, was the exact opposite of what one had expected of them. So it was really no surprise that their usual habit of retiring early was broken the one time we wanted them to do just that. This happened one evening when we were giving a dinner party prior to visiting the theatre. In spite of yawning their heads off at 6 p.m. they woke up when guests started to arrive and began to join in the fun. Nothing would entice them back to their cage. Solomon would come to hand all right, but if one approached the cage he took off again; as for Sheba, it was just impossible to get near her – even the broomstick was rejected. We tried putting our coats on. This usually made Solomon go to his travel cage for he loved an outing, but that night he was not to be so fooled. Since neither was prepared to co-operate it took a good twenty minutes to get both caged. Once they were in we covered the cage with an old blanket hoping that darkness would prevent squabbles. It did, and even when it was removed on our return neither bird stirred. Well we, if not they, were exhausted and for the first time ever we had missed a play's opening lines.

On a grey November day, after Sheba had been with us for just over three months, the Curator called with the news that London Zoo's new parrot house was complete and he would be ready to receive the conures the following week. So, sadly, our happy if oft-times hectic relationship drew quietly to a close. Yet Solomon and Sheba's very joyful 'togetherness' since they started life at London Zoo has been ample compensation for the awful sense of loss I felt at that time.

Chapter 9

'Life at London Zoo'

When the time came to take Solomon and Sheba to the Zoo I felt something of a traitor, for I still had many doubts as to how they would settle in. Of course, I had the assurance that if they pined I should have them back, which made it easier. All the same, not really trusting myself to drive there, I took a taxi. The two conures travelling together in the top half of the large cage, were restless, but there was no attempt to squabble.

The Curator, waiting to receive them at the doors of the re-converted Parrot House, made a good job of reassuring me that they would soon settle down. In fact, it was he who had kindly suggested that I take Solomon and Sheba up several weeks before the new house opened to the public, which meant I could visit them frequently, thereby making the break gradually and in consequence as painlessly as possible. I must say here that without exception, the entire staff of the Parrot House were most sympathetic and helpful towards this end. So it was not long before I was completely confident that both Solomon and Sheba were going to be very happy there.

Sheba seemed more upset by the move than Solomon was, but then he was used to change. Even so, as soon as a young keeper opened their cage to transfer them to their allotted quarters,

Solomon catapulted out, making a bee-line for my shoulder. There he stayed while the Curator showed me round the rather bleak building, and explained something of their routine work.

The cage allotted to them was, thankfully, large enough for even two humans to walk round in; $8' \times 6' \times 8'$ high. But I knew it would seem very cell-like to Solomon at least, who was used to complete freedom. However, after I had been in with him for about half-an-hour I had him swinging from one of the branches and eating the odd seed. Sheba, alas, was very distressed and because of her damaged feet, she had difficulty in keeping her balance when she landed on the freely swinging branches that their cage was equipped with. Thus she clung to the netted side and let off steam vocally.

Having spent nearly an hour with them, I left for work with a heavy heart, but I really did not do much before visiting them again that evening. Neither bird had touched its seeds. This was more than likely due to the food containers being at ground level rather than high up, where they were used to having them, because both Solomon and Sheba ate well when I hand fed them. Solomon had his on my shoulder, but left of his own accord when he'd had enough, settling fairly close to Sheba, who had at last managed to perch, if precariously, on one of the swinging branches. Both began making their sleepy noises, so having given each of them a titbit I took my departure in a slightly lighter frame of mind than I had done that morning.

Next day I returned at lunchtime and was happily surprised to see the two conures cuddled close. Sheba's head rested against Solomon's bosom, while he gently preened her neck feathers. The keepers had found them thus that morning. It was truly a delight to watch them and although Solomon flew down to me as soon as I entered their cage, he quickly returned to Sheba's side. Obviously their transfer to neutral territory was the final push Solomon needed to give in to Sheba's shameless chasing! In fact both birds seemed so content I let a full forty-eight hours elapse before paying them another visit. Sheba having 'Got Her Man' was noticeably blooming, and since Solomon had teased out her feather buds she looked really pretty. There could be little doubt that she, at any rate, was by then content with her lot.

At first Solomon was quite evidently still as pleased to see me as he was to be with Sheba, remaining jealous of any attention I gave her. This resulted in his chivvying her to the far end of the branch a few minutes after my arrival, before flying down to my shoulder. But it was not long before his attitude began to change and he henceforth showed a marked possessiveness towards her. This manifested itself one day when Sheba, having been shoo-ed off, began getting friendly with one of the Canary-winged parrakeets living in an adjoining cage. When Solomon noticed this flirting he flew over in fury and attacked the poor thing as best he could, through the dividing bars, before chasing an astonished Sheba back to their branch. Actually he was thereby exhibiting a marked tendency of these conures, who are normally friendly with other birds, to become decidedly aggressive when truly paired with one of their own kind. Thus, to my relief, it was clear he had at last started transferring his affections from me to Sheba, so much so that I can well imagine him championing her against the most unlikely odds.

Solomon gave an even clearer demonstration of his love for Sheba when, on my last visit before the public opening, I stood just beyond their aviary door, with Solomon on my shoulder, to see whether or not he was really happy enough to want to stay. I soon had a very definite answer. On hearing Sheba's cries of protest he flew straight back in again and immediately cuddled close to her. His actions removed any lingering doubts as to whether the two of them would settle happily into life at London Zoo. So I went on my way with a relatively easy mind about them.

Hence I was all the more disturbed at his behaviour when I first visited them after the house was open to the public and I could no longer go inside their cage. This somehow bothered Solomon, in particular, who kept frantically bowing up and down (an action of parrots which usually signifies frustration of some sort or their desire to get out). He then began crashing against the bars dividing us, while Sheba too began distressed bowing motions.

It was just as well that the 'No Feeding' rule was not in force at that time, for eventually both calmed down when I produced their titbits of apple, grape and Brazil nut. It seemed that their anxiety was not just 'cupboard love', for having finished his apple Solomon demanded that his pate be scratched, a sure sign that he felt rather sorry for himself. Sheba too began rubbing her head along the branch nearest me in a soppy manner.

Naturally I was rather upset by this turn of events. It seemed that after all they had not settled as well as I thought. Nevertheless after three visits in the painful manner described above, both birds had accepted the procedure as normal, and Solomon no longer required his head scratched. Even so, they remained eager for their titbits, Sheba still taking hers from my fingers in a decidedly nervous manner, but thanking me in a particularly sweet way when she got back to her perch. She always finished her piece to the very last drop of juice or particle of nut, while Solomon would discard his half way through and come looking for more. Since they both gained so much pleasure from these offerings it was therefore an especially sad day for me when the ban on feeding all Zoo animals came into force.

Although, like me, I am sure that both public and animals alike are sorely disappointed at the new ruling, visitors will perhaps agree, if reluctantly, that there has long been a need for some form of control on 'Social' feeding, that is normally such a pleasure for recipient and donor. Reasons for the ban are many: firstly unsuitable food, thoughtlessly given in spite of warnings, if only by a few, resulted tragically in death for a number of animals, some rare and costly, while a great many more became quite ill.

Over the years this indiscriminate feeding has caused considerable financial loss to the Zoo. Also the authorities believe that it has had a detrimental effect on successful breeding. They are, therefore, hoping that the new controlled, balance diets will be a help in improving their breeding record, intending this to go hand in hand with their policy of conservation.

Still it must be rather awful to be continually stared at and receive no compensatory titbit. To be fair, it isn't all the public's fault; creatures like pelicans and elephants have been known to snatch and even swallow a handy coat button, camera or handbag, if some more palatable offering was not forthcoming! It is indeed a problem and even solutions that would at first seem more logical, such as wholesale selling of suitable food, e.g. peanuts for monkeys, bananas for elephants, fish for pelicans, etc., in the vicinity of their quarters, have their drawbacks, in that the less lively, or more nervous animals would receive none, while others would receive too much, for some like humans are greedy and seem not to know when they have had enough, so at least the Zoo have now got a definite control over the amount of food taken by the animals and have therefore managed to stem the loss of those dying from fatty degeneration of the heart.

London's Zoo's conservation programme, whose ideals will be welcomed by all animal lovers whether advocates of Zoos in general or not, has affectionately become known as their 'Marriage Bureau Service', one aspect of this scheme being co-operation with the Federation of Zoos of Great Britain and Ireland, whose headquarters is actually at London Zoo. Step one is arranging an exchange of rare animals between zoos who have them, during their normal mating season, e.g. the sad non-romance of those notorious, popular pandas Chi-Chi and An-An. Later, when numbers have been increased by such 'marriages' that are successful and where sufficient breeding pairs are established, it is hoped to repopulate areas of the world where the particular species is becoming extinct, always providing, of course, that the original cause of decline has been discovered and eliminated. Shamefully, man is all too often to blame for this sorry state of affairs! Ideally, areas so repopulated will then be designated as Wildlife Sanctuaries.

Ban on feeding or not, I feel that the most serious deterrent to successful breeding in most zoos is lack of suitable accommodation. The majority of animals and birds require a good measure of privacy as well as space in which to propagate, and because London Zoo's rebuilding programme was badly retarded during the war years, they still have considerable leeway to make up. However, although I feel that certain animals, such as elephants, are very badly done by for space even in their new quarters, they make continual progress in rehousing.

Anyway, I sincerely hope there will be sufficient funds from the sale of this book to endow at least one suitable breeding aviary for parrots, which I feel might perhaps be better established at their country property, Whipsnade. Alternatively, I should like to see these funds contribute towards the cost of sending an ornithologist, under the auspices of the Zoo, to carry out helpful and sadly lacking research in this field, on the South American, Indian and Australian continents.

Incidentally budgerigars breed particularly well at the Zoo, being ideally housed in a very attractive aviary, which was initially of a 'Homing' variety, prettily set on a verdant island. It stands as a memorial to the 12th Duke of Bedford, from the Society of Aviculturalists. There could hardly be a more fitting tribute, since the Duke was the first to set up 'homing' aviaries in Britain. When I first saw them it was truly a delight to watch these 'budgies' flying freely out of their aviary to play happily in surrounding trees and plants, or returning 'indoors' for food, often taking nesting material with them. So it is indeed sad that because of interference from the visiting public, and also the risk of them contracting diseases from sparrows and pigeons, the aviary is now a closed one. Even so, it is still one of the best in the Zoo. Happily the public can still see free-flying birds at Len Hill's, Bourton-on-the-Water 'Birdland', in the Cotswolds, where apart from keeping many larger species at complete liberty Mr Hill, a fellow of the Zoological Society, is developing a strain of 'Homing' Parrakeets.

As to breeding with regard to Solomon and Sheba, they had become so attentive in manner towards each other that it was taken as a sign of such intent. So, in early January they were given a plain-fronted standard nest box. Having ignored its presence for a week or two they took to it for sleeping in, yet showed no other sign of nesting.

One of the young keepers suggested that the box be lined with a peat sod or moss, but this was not done, mainly I think, because it was considered that the box would become too hot in the artificially heated Parrot House. Personally I was always rather sorry that this suggestion wasn't carried out, especially now that they are outside, because it would seem to approximate more nearly to the conditions of their natural nesting site, which, unlike the tree hollows favoured by most parrots, is an arboreal termite's nest, that is, in fact, quite humid and soft at its centre. With Sheba's damaged feet I am sure she would appreciate the extra comfort of a turf. The external similarity of these termite nests to wasp nests may have accounted for Solomon's at one time uncomfortable interest in the latter, while we were living in Arizona, an interest that so aggravated its inhabitants that the Fire Brigade was eventually detailed to remove the lot!

Incidentally, roosting in the nest site prior to mating seems to be normal procedure with these conures, as according to Hardy's observations, both free and captive birds spent a considerable period before nesting using their chosen sites to roost in, while ignoring them during the day. He believes that in this way the birds allow ample time for the termites to seal themselves off from the main nesting cavity and the tunnel leading into it.

I was very happy when, in May, Solomon and Sheba were transferred to their own outdoor aviary, $15' \times 8' \times 10'$ high, plus an attached indoor cubicle $6' \times 4' \times 10'$ high, where in cold weather they get warmth from the main building, through the connecting window, which is left open at night. As there was by then no doubt at all that both conures were completely happy I cut my visits down to one a month, and over the Spring season stayed away altogether, hoping that if undisturbed by such visits they would get on with producing their young. I don't think either of them is well enough equipped to start in the wild again and as long as they are captive this set-up seems ideal for them and all the other birds who enjoy it, although I do feel that these aviaries lack the seclusion that might perhaps finally encourage them to breed.

Maybe the placing of branches around the nest boxes, bare though they be of leaves, would give them the necessary feeling of security. Parrots being highly strung as well as intelligent, require a good measure of privacy to mate and breed successfully, which sensitivity I'm sure most of us can fully appreciate, for I doubt that there are many of their human friends who do not share these same delicate inhibitions! Actually I should add that many improvements along these lines are currently being made. For instance, Solomon and Sheba's near neighbours, a pair of Keas, now have a super 'rockery' in which to play and/or breed. The Kea's delight in it is so very plain for all to see that this in itself must surely compensate the curator in no small way, for the trouble he has taken in establishing it.

Be that as it may, by August it was clear that for some reason the cuddlesome frolics of Solomon and Sheba were purely platonic – either that, or Solomon is a 'little Lord Fauntleroy' blissfully unaware of the facts of life! Even so, their keepers are still hopeful of obtaining progeny, since similar species have been known to need two to three years without disturbance before breeding. This would seem to tie in with Hardy's observations, viz. 'Aviculturists are generally agreed that in order to obtain successful breeding results from the Petz's conure, in captivity, one must isolate the potential pair in a secluded aviary not less than 8' wide, 12' high × 24' long. Moreover breeding may not occur even then until the birds have been allowed to grow accustomed to their aviaries for two to three years.' Apparently this is so even if they continue to go through various courtship displays at the appropriate season.

Meanwhile all the staff do their best to keep them happy and encourage them to raise a family. This includes the touching efforts of the young keepers who, in their spare time, have fashioned from bark an encouragingly 'natural' looking face to their standard nest box. Here again the observations of Mr Hardy might well prove of interest and perhaps help, since he has experimented with regard to favoured nesting material amongst his captive flock consisting of fifteen birds.

His birds were offered a choice of standard nest box and two mock termatoria, one made from cork and the other from styrafoam, the latter having its outer surface dyed brown. All birds ignored the nest box and digging started on both termatoria. However the styrafoam model was abandoned as soon as the birds came across the white granules. Apart from the white material reflecting too much light (for conures like dark cavities) they may have disliked its texture. Anyhow the cork version was fully accepted and the birds seemed to find it fairly easy to tunnel into. Since they took to the latter Hardy supplied them with a ready-made cork nesting box, simulating tunnel angles and the nursery cavity as near to the natural as possible, but incorporating a lid, as per standard boxes. Apparently this was used successfully.

All keepers at the Zoo regard their work more as a 'vocation', which it really seems to be, for much of their routine work is tedious and sometimes unpleasant. Yet they manage to make light of it, and in spite of full, busy days, they amazingly always seem to find time to pander to the individual whims of their various charges. Happily this admirable trait runs throughout the staff and it is this build-up of careful, individual attention given by each keeper, which, I am sure, makes all the difference to the birds' mental wellbeing and therefore aids considerably in keeping them generally fit and content.

A normal Zoo day begins with unpleasant cleaning chores. First item on the agenda is to sweep and scrub all cage floors, perches and cage bars. Then comes cleaning of food and water containers and the soft bark logs. This daily hygiene, essential to the successful care of all animals, is particularly important where so many are housed under one roof. The cage floors are finally damped down and re-sanded, at which point young keepers have fun with those birds who are particularly fond of a shower. On warm days all parrots housed indoors are sprayed – normally twice a week in the summer – but, pandering to those who are partial to a daily bath (like my two water-babies), keepers oblige by giving them a few light puffs with the spray. Those birds who do fancy being wet get into the strangest, most amusing contortions to attract attention at this time and also to ensure that they get well sprayed all over.

Meanwhile various foodstuffs are being mixed. Quite a problem this, since many parrots have just as many fads and fancies regarding their diets as we humans do, quite apart from the basic differences required by the various species. Fruit, which is placed on top of each seed dish, is varied from day to day, say lettuce and apple on Monday, grapes and peas the next day, and so on, depending, of course, on what is in season, but helping to ensure that at least once a week even the fussiest parrot gets some favourite fruit.

Quite apart from Brazil and other nuts being a necessary part of a macaw's diet, and more because they love them so much, the headkeeper will, after he has finished dishing out the seeds, go through a touching ritual, handing a Brazil nut to each individual macaw housed in the internal aviaries. Each special treat is avidly received and I am sure is much more appreciated than if they were left to find the nuts amongst their other rations. This then is another example of the affectionate interest keepers take in their charges. Of course, while he feeds and chats to each bird the keeper runs a practised eye over all of them, making sure they are well, and taking appropriate action should any appear to be 'off colour'. Old parrots are pampered with a mash made from wholemeal bread, milk and honey, which also supplements the diets of breeding pairs.

Amongst the mess cleared out of all habitats each day are horrifying examples of thoughtlessness by some of the visiting public. Rejected flashbulbs and the remains of lighted cigarettes are but two of the really dangerous objects to be found littering cages throughout the Zoo. It seems incredible that the public are unaware of the possibly tragic results of such carelessness. Equally inconceivable is thinking these acts are sadistic deliberation, yet one or other they must surely be.

By the end of September I again started visiting Solomon and Sheba more frequently, mainly for the purpose of making the accompanying illustrations. Oddly enough, I never seemed to have the time to do many of these when they were actually with me. A few months in the open air has done much to improve their condition. Both are now svelt, while their plumage shines as brightly as their eyes, fully justifying the derivation of their scientific name, which is – pertaining to Sirius – the brightest star in the sky, hence the centre of attraction (which, of course, they delight in being).

Their more natural way of life has, it seems, irrevocably erased the desire that Solomon had heretofore shown for my company, which is of course as it should be. In fact, when the Head keeper first let me into their aviary both Solomon and Sheba flew, in evident fright, to the netting farthest from us. However, I took no notice of them but started arranging my drawing implements, and it wasn't long before both had recognised me, and having flown across to a nearby branch, began a chorus of greeting calls.

Solomon approached very close, staring deeply at me with thoughtful introspection. He gave my proffered finger a quick,

gentle 'handshake', then moved back to Sheba and preened a few of her feathers. But quite obviously his mind was not on this task. He continued to gaze at me, the look in his eye being almost unfathomable, a mixture of puzzled curiosity. Quite suddenly he gave an ear-splitting shriek, dive-bombed my shoulder, and rested there lightly for a moment. It was, I think, his last concession to a far-off, albeit happy memory, as if he were saying 'I haven't forgotten you, but I much prefer it here, with Sheba.' A quick dab of his beak against my cheek and Solomon was gone. In the next instant he was, quite rightly, snuggled close to his bride. But it was, as you may imagine, a moment highly charged with emotion.

Having given her spouse a good biffing by way of a ticking-off for his momentary desertion, Sheba relented, and for more than half an hour the pair kept up a series of goofy, cuddlesome frolics that were truly a delight to watch. Tender dressing of each other's feathers was interspersed with playful boxing bouts that led to their interlocking beaks, while they performed elaborate courtship bowing to each other. Then they would sit for a while, quite still, but still with their beaks interlocked. Occasionally their tongues would appear to tickle the other's; oddly enough this was often accompanied by 'kissing' noises. Then back to dressing each other's feathers; meanwhile they kept up a continuous, pleasant-toned chuckling of 'sweet nothings', while the expression in their eyes was thoroughly soppy.

Later they flew, as one, to their nesting-box where Sheba momentarily disappeared inside while Solomon, though peering in after her, did not follow but sat on the perch at its entrance, where Sheba shortly joined him. When she did so, Solomon rested his head on her neck to take a nap. He was not allowed to snooze for long, however, because although it was clear that Sheba still longed to be really friendly, she remained far too nervous to become so. Therefore she was unrelaxed at being so close to where I sat, the box being within my arm's reach, so, although for a while she rested her head against Solomon's bosom, she kept a wary eye on me, looking suspicious every time I made a slight move merely to wash out a paintbrush, or take up some fresh colour. The trouble was, I think, my intent gaze upon them both as I sketched, since no bird, however friendly, likes to be stared at. Even Solomon at his tamest used to turn his back if one watched him intently for any length of time. In the end, when Sheba could bear it no longer, she prodded Solomon awake and chivvied him back to a branch at the centre of their aviary.

Sheba obviously felt more confident with Solomon awake and

alert beside her, for when I handed both a grape, she watched Solomon taking his from my fingers and then moved forward to get hers, which I had intended sticking on a twig, but she grabbed it nervously out of my hand before I was able to do so.

Sheba, as usual, devoured even the skin of her grape, then flew down to the ground to finish off the half that Solomon had typically discarded. She looked ridiculously small and somehow terribly vulnerable, picking her way through the unkempt grass. I noticed she jumped nervously as a butterfly fluttered past, lightly brushing her head, just as I had seen Solomon, on many occasions, flinching foolishly at flies, etc.

I had entered their aviary at 8 a.m., which enabled me to concentrate completely on observing the birds. It was just as well that I had these two hours in hand before the public began wandering through the grounds, because once they did, they did their best to distract me with good-natured jests, such as: 'Cor, I didn't expect to see a "Bird" like you here' – and, in spite of 'No Feeding' signs, came numerous offers of 'Have a pea-nut Ducks!'

Naturally enough, although I am truly delighted with the way Solomon and Sheba have settled in so happily at London Zoo, I still miss having them around. It seems strange that they are no longer my responsibility and, though they are very obviously extremely well-cared for, I still, on occasion, feel anxious as regards their welfare, particularly when heavy fog cloaks the city, or blizzards occur, or we suffer other such inclement weather. However, I am indeed thankful that the answers to my enquiries on these occasions have generally been reassuring. For instance, I understand that the morning following an especially heavy blizzard the two of them were playing happily amidst the snow, just as if they hailed from Arctic regions and not the tropics!

Although I am adding a chapter encompassing the ecology of Petz's conures, various beak comparisons and suggested reference books, the actual story of Solomon and Sheba, for the time being at any rate, ends here, I think you will agree on a fairly happy note. Still, I hope that one day I will be able to pen a sequal to this story, concerning their progeny, if not their further adventures.

Chapter 10

General Ecology of the Petz's Conure

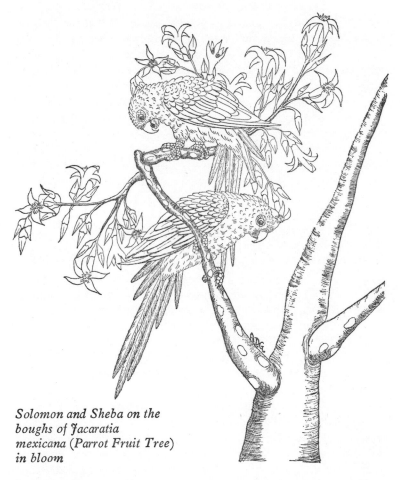

Solomon and Sheba on the boughs of Jacaratia mexicana (Parrot Fruit Tree) in bloom

In their wild state Petz's conures feed largely on the fruit of the tree *Jacaratia mexicana*, previously known as *Pileus conica*. Its common name is 'Parrot Fruit Tree', which is apt, since the tree not only supplies these conures with food, but helps to protect them from their natural arch enemy – man excepted – the Grey Hawk, *Buteo nitidus*. My drawing of Solomon and Sheba on the cover indicates the protection afforded by the colour of this fruit alone.

The phenomenon is further illustrated by the following extract from Bebe's *Two Bird Lovers in Mexico*, published 1849: — 'These little parrakeets were not shy, but very watchful and when frightened they always flew to a curious looking tree, which, though bare of leaves was sparsely covered with an odd looking, long, four sided fruit of a green colour. Under such circumstances they all alighted together and unlike their usual sociable custom of perching in pairs, they scattered all over the tree, stood very upright and remained motionless. From a distance of only 50 feet we found it impossible to distinguish parrakeet from fruit. This silent trust in the protective resemblance of the fruit was all the more remarkable when we remembered the frantic shrieking which these birds always set up at the approach of danger when they happened to be caught away from one of these Parrot Fruit Trees.'

Obviously the above incident took place when the fruit was ripe. I have been unable to find any account of the conures' behaviour as regards their 'silent trust' in this tree at other times of the year. Albeit their passion for the ripe fruit is so great they seem to put up with having their beaks gummed up and feathers soiled with its sticky juice. This is, of course, completely contradictory to their normal instinct, which borders on the fussy, as regards keeping their plumage clean.

The fruit of the *Jacaratia mexicana* is closely related to papaya and its flesh is much like it, being sweet, orangy in colour and scattered with rough black seeds. Its external appearance could be likened to a green pepper, but varies more in shape. Normally bullnose, it is sometimes long and grotesquely twisted, but is always divided into five obvious sections. On average it grows to a length of just above six inches, while its top circumference is approximately three inches. The outer skin is basically green or yellow, more usually the former, erratically streaked with blue and charcoal, while some have patches of orange and yet others of brownish olive.

The Parrot Fruit Tree is odd and strangely shaped in many

ways. Aproximately forty feet high, its bark is smooth, light grey and thick at the base. Its wood is very soft and the trunk, largely pith, tapers upward in cone-like fashion, dividing into unusually few, but heavy branches. The branches have a scabby appearance, marking the points where the fruit has previously hung on thick, umbilical-like stems. Leaves are deciduous and clustered at the ends of branches, with five to seven obovate, acuminate leaflets. The tree is, however, completely barren of leaves when its fruit is ripe. At that time only a few straggly twigs remain, giving it a dionysiac appearance. Its dioecious flowers are extremely pretty and delicate, with staminate in terminal, axillary panicles of pale yellow. Terminal pistillate petals are white, while pedunculate petals, four centimetres long, are pale green. The corolla, two centimetres long, is white. Stamens, ten centimetres long, are deep yellow.

Sadly, though not altogether surprisingly, I have never been able to obtain any 'Parrot Fruit' for Solomon or Sheba in this country. They had to make do with mangoes and papayas. However, I do wonder that zoos and reserves in general don't organise a tie-up with botanical societies, like Kew, in growing such rarities for the benefit of their inmates in particular, and research in general, especially since such a link could lead to the possibility of the British public being able to enjoy a close at hand sight of animals such as Australia's cuddlesome Koala bears whose staple diet is Eucalyptus leaves.

Owners of tropical fruit groves naturally tend to view parrots, conures and like species with a somewhat jaundiced eye, but it may be that Mexican farmers are untroubled by the presence of Petz's conures at harvest time. At any rate I have never heard of any complaints against them in this respect. Certainly neither Solomon nor Sheba would ever eat Indian corn in any form, either raw or cooked, although it is, of course, a food that most Psittacine birds enjoy. Likewise both my birds rejected peanuts as though they were poison, but savoured almost any nut from the American continents, e.g. Pecans, Walnuts, Royal Hawaiian Macadamia nuts, and, needless to say, Brazils. Regarding Brazils, they seemed almost as keen on the inner shell as on the nut itself, crushing it very finely with evident enjoyment, presumably eating this in place of grit. However, I make this observation solely from the habits of Solomon and Sheba who, no matter how hungry they were, refused to eat their seeds should grit be mixed with them, and if aught else failed to show us what they thought of the stuff, they used their beaks as shovels to rid the dish of its entire contents.

As to other forest fruits that go to make up the diet of Petz's conures in their natural habitat, they feast on figs, small fleshy podlike fruits of the scrubby Myrrh *Bursera sp* and, according to Hardy, on the following as well:—'At Tehuantepec, on the flat coastal plain, the parrakeets were seen frequenting scrubbier vegetation called Scrubthorn. There, however, they spent diurnal hours in the plantations of mangoes, coconut palms and other tropical fruit, adjacent to the town.' He also notes that Petz's conures never roost in their feeding grounds, but travel up to a mile away to sleep in the forests, even returning there for daytime snoozes. Mentioning food that is readily available at nesting time Hardy says:—'Seemingly only pantiallate matter in liquid, regurgitable form, fed to nestlings included small fleshy fruits of unidentified trees and flowers of a scandent shrub, *Comretum farinosura* (family *Terminaliaceae*) in full bloom.' The flowers of this woody vine are bright orange and full of nectar. The flower parts are fleshy and when pressed between the fingers assume a gummy consistency.

He goes on to say that he successfully hand-reared some captive young on these flowers by mashing them up with milk. Feeding was by a plastic dropper and Gaping was induced by pressure at each side of the lower bill. Apparently these fledglings would not gape in response to any other stimuli. This last piece of information seems an important point to remember for anyone attempting to breed these conures, since all the accounts I have read where breeding in captivity has been realised have been followed by a report of the parents deserting their young from anything after a few days to a few weeks after hatching. Actually, once the fledgling is able to leave the nest it should be possible to wean it from dropper to spoon-feeding. It is, however, a process that is very time-consuming since at first it must be carried out at least once every hour and, as with feeding children, a great deal of patience is required. The experience should, however, be a rewarding one, and almost guarantees a very tame adult parrot.

Incidentally, I noted with considerable interest, whilst reading one of Mr Hardy's papers, that some of his valuable field studies on Petz's conures were carried out in the vicinity of Chiapas, because this is very close to the spot where I first saw them. I regret now that at the time they were to me but part of the general landscape, as my concentration was fully devoted to studies at a jungle survival centre, the outcome of which, as yet untried, I sincerely hope may still prove useful should I be fortunate enough to return one day to South America's unexplored jungles.

Although I have written this in 'layman's' language the following section on the breeding of Petz's Conures is almost entirely based on Mr J. W. Hardy's recorded experiences subsequent to his intensive study of these birds both in their natural habitat and under captive circumstances. (See also chapter 9.)

As I've already mentioned, Petz's conures utilise arboreal termitaries of the termite *Nasutitermes* for nesting sites, the host plant generally being an oak tree. These termitaries, roughly ovular in shape, known locally as 'Ballos', are sometimes enormous, occasionally even overshadowing a man, but their average size is generally far smaller. Both male and female conures take part in the excavation of their chosen ballo, though the major part of this work is done by the male, especially in the early stages. They begin digging low on the side of the ballo and direct a tunnel, from eight inches to one foot long and approximately two-and-a-half inches in diameter, upwards at an angle. On reaching the friable central part, the birds veer downwards to form a 'nursery' which, when complete, is roughly spherical in shape.

Normally any breaks in the ballo immediately stimulate soldier and worker termites to repair the damage, but for some reason, as yet unknown, they very soon leave the conures' work undisturbed, merely sealing off any of their own labyrinth of canals that enters into the Petz's' tunnel or nursery cavity. Oddly enough, after the conures have vacated the nest, termites will often return to using that section while conures will never use a ballo that has been completely deserted by the termites. Apparently the conures seem only mildly irritated by any termites they encounter on their initial dig, shaking them off with a rapid head-waggling movement, and just as the termites make no attempt to attack the conures or their vulnerable naked fledglings (yet inflict ferocious bites on any other creature that invades their territory), so the conures leave the termites at peace once their digging is complete and certainly make no attempt to eat them. Thus there exists between them what on the surface appears to be a curiously negative relationship. Yet there must be more to it than meets the eye since Petz's conures seem to be wholly dependent on termite ballos for their own nests. It has been postulated that the Petz's is not capable of maintaining population without symbiotic association with the termite; one reason, perhaps, why they are so difficult to breed in captivity.

For a period of approximately one week following the excavating work the pair of conures do not visit the ballo at all, possibly allowing due time for the termites to vacate the nursery area and seal off their own channels leading into it. Following this comes a period in which the pair use the nest to roost in at night, but still ignore it during the day. Next come frequent attempts at successful copulation. The female solicits by raising her tail and the male will often preen her lower tail coverts before mounting. I have occasionally seen Solomon and Sheba do just this since they have been at London Zoo, and take it as a hopeful sign that they will eventually get around to breeding. Unlike the majority of birds, mounting is but partial with these conures, the male placing only one foot on the female's back, while perching beside her.

Only the female incubates the eggs, but the male still enters the nest to feed her and to roost. Their average clutch is three to five eggs, of a dull white colour. Short and subliptical in shape, their size is approximately 2.67 cm. x 2.03 cm. They are usually laid at one day intervals, and incubation takes from twenty-six to thirty days. On hatching, shells are generally removed from the nest and both parents commence feeding of the chicks.

As already noted, flowers of the shrub *Combretum farinosum* are apparently an integral constituent of the parents' vegitaceous regurgitant. The young, at hatching, are covered in down. A two day old chick weighs approximately two grams and its size is approximately forty-five millimetres. They are altricial and anisodactyl. Their first plumage emerges by the end of the first week. They are feathered by the middle of the third week and are then zygodactyl. Their plumage is identical to that of the adults, the only difference being that their circumorbital skin is whitish and their irrides are brown.

The following general and scientific description of Petz's conures covers:—*Eupsittula canicularis, Aratinga canicularis,*

General Ecology of the Petz's Conure

Canicularis canicularis, Conurus canicularis, and *Canicularis eburnirostrum.*

PETZ'S CONURES are arboreal. They are capable climbers and frugivorus. They are non-migratory. Males are monogamous, but since these conures are highly sociable, birds of both sexes may also have so-called 'homosexual' relations within the limits of their own flock. True pairs remain very devoted to each other throughout the year and not just during the mating season. Captive birds make no attempt to breed until they are at least two years old.

HABITAT: Tropical deciduous and scrub-thorn forests of Pacific mountain slopes and lowlands, ranging from Sinola, Mexico to Costa Rica; Petz's conures are not to be found breeding outside the geographic range of the termite *Eutermes (Nasutitermes) nigriceps.*

ADULT LENGTH: 9½ inches. Their tail measurement accounts for half this length, while the folded wings cover one third.

CULMEN *or* UPPER MANDIBLE: Fleshy white, stout, macaw-like, shortish and in the male it is sharply hooked. In the female the culmen is more finely formed and less curved. The ceres bulges on both and is lightly feathered. LOWER MANDIBLE: Sides are brownish black, while the underenath is fleshy white. TONGUE: Smooth, thick, fleshy and black. NAKED ORBITAL SKIN: Yellow in adults, whitish in fledglings. Short, fine, black lashes surround the orofice. IRRIDES: Yellow in adults, dark reddish-brown in fledglings. PUPILS: Dark reddish-black. BINOCULAR VISION: 6°–10°. TOES: Anisodactyl in fledglings, zygodactyl in adults. TARSI: Short, and like the toes, are covered with tiny, charcoal-grey granular scales. PTERNA (pads under feet): A pale pinkish colour.

The charm of the Petz's conure lies not only in its engaging personality, but also in the beauty of its plumage, whose colouring is as follows: —

CROWN AND LORES: Dusty French blue. NAPE, HIND-NECK, BACK (mantle), SCAPULARS AND RUMP: A shimmering, almost iridescent jade green. AURICULARS, MALAR REGION (cheeks), CHIN, THROAT AND BREAST: Yellowy-brown olive green. BELLY, SIDE FLANKS (area covered by folded wings), UPPER AND LOWER TAIL COVERTS: Bright yellow-green. *N.B.*: Quills divide all flight and tail feathers as regards their shadings, e.g. from green to turquoise, or olivaceous yellow to silvery grey, etc. etc. TOP OF OUTER PRIMARIES: Green, edged with glittering turquoise. REMAINDER OF PRIMARIES:

Bluish-green with charcoal tips. TOP OF SECONDARIES: French blue, the outer webs being narrowly edged with green. TOP OF TERTIARIES: Shimmering jade green. UNDERNEATH OF ALL FLIGHTS: Charcoal grey, shaded to a light grey at the outer webs. UNDERNEATH OF TOP HALF OF WINGS: Bright olivaceous yellow. GREATER UNDER WING COVERTS: Charcoal grey with yellowish edges. TOP OF TAIL FEATHERS: Jade green, with the TWO CENTRAL TAIL FEATHERS turning to French blue about halfway towards the tip. UNDERNEATH OF ALL FEATHERS are olivaceous yellow on the inner webs, while outer webs are silvery grey.

PLUMULES under the abdominal, throat, neck and back feathers are pale grey, fluffy feathers known as powder-down, consisting of soft and friable down whose main shaft continually disintegrates, giving off miniscule particles of a fine greyish-white powdery substance, which aids all parrots in keeping their feathers clean. By the way, dust from the disintegrated down increases in no small way the mess made by parrots if they are kept indoors. Powder-down is by no means common to all birds, but it is also found in herons, toucans and bowerbirds. Probably powder-down also helps to keep them warm, and this could well be a factor that aids many parrots to flourish in British climes, for provided they are acclimatised gradually and given a draught-free shelter, the majority of parrots, Petz's conures included, appear to be quite hardy, especially where they are kept in pairs (so they can huddle together for warmth) and are either at complete liberty, or in large aviaries that allow lengthy warming flights. In really severe weather, however, they should be returned to lightly heated indoor accommodation, particularly at night. They will also tend to eat quite a bit more.

Feathers in general replace scales of reptilians from which it is believed birds are descended. Feathers prevent loss of body heat by radiation, and in most birds develop in definite tracts or pterylae. An oil gland near the base of the tail is believed to help in keeping feathers waterproof. The tail is used for steering when flying, a brake when alighting, for birds like parrots and woodpeckers, and as a support when climbing. Tail feathers grow on 'a plate of bone' known as the pygostyle, which is the compressed remains of the vertebrae of the long reptile tail, but now only little discs, or rectices, can be seen. Wings are a modification of the arm and hand. Traces of only three fingers now remain. The primaries grow on joined fingers, secondaries are attached to the forearm, from wrist to elbow. Wings are strengthened for flight by the development of breast muscles attached to the Sternum.

EAR: Far better developed than in humans as regards both hearing and balance – so essential in flight. But although birds have acute and highly developed reception and therefore a faster response than humans to distant sounds, their frequency range, 40–14,000 cycles is more limited than ours. However, their sense of frequency discrimination, within this range, probably equals that of man. Since they can distinguish the same sounds as we can it is one reason, perhaps for their mimicry capabilities.

BRAIN: Brain sizes vary enormously amongst different species of birds, but logically enough it is those with outstanding intelligence that have an especially large forebrain. Just as with humans, whose intelligence is controlled in the same manner, it follows that parrots and crows, acknowledged to be the most intelligent birds, have the largest brains relative to weight in the bird kingdom. It is an interesting parallel, which could, I presume, account for their misery in confined captivity.

FOSSILS: The earliest known parrot remains is an early miocene fossil *Psittacus verreauxii*, discovered by A. Milne-Edwards during the mid-1800s in the tertiary deposits of Saint-Gérard-le-Puy Langy, in the Allier district of France. It is said to present much anology with certain African species, especially *Psittacus erithacus* of Senegal and South Africa, with whose physiology the Petz's conure seems to have a great deal in common.

BEAKS: Conures, like all other parrots, have their strong upper mandible hinged to their skulls, the consequent flexibility being useful for climbing purposes as well as for eating. But since, even within their dietary differences, the size and shape of parrots' beaks vary so tremendously, I thought it might be interesting to include a few examples here, comparing two or three from each of the main dietary groups that are basically as follows:—Fruit and Nut eaters, Nut and Seed eaters, Seed and Grain eaters, Nectar eaters, Tuberous Vegetable eaters, and although grubs, insects, etc. are supplementary to most, in one or two instances these make up the bulk of a diet.

FRUIT AND NUT EATERS:

In nut-eating parrots the upper bill is curved down and inwards at the tip to hold the nuts while they are being crushed by the lower mandible. Further, in Petz's conures, as with other nut-eating parrots, the upper mandible is serrated on the underside of its front prominence with transverse, 'rasp-like' ridges, which means that these parrots are able partially to masticate their food, a function which is normally left entirely to the gizzard in other birds and is one reason perhaps why they seem able to do without grit. For comparison of fruit and nut eaters I have taken the beaks of the Petz's conure and the Hyacinthine macaw, both from South America, plus an illustration only of the Blue and Yellow macaw.

Hyacinthine Macaw: Anodorhynus hyacinthinus: If kept as pets, all macaws need a great deal of attention and affection from their owners, as well as plenty of exercise. Generally friendly, they often become quite savage while breeding. They vary in size from thirteen inches (Hahn's macaw), to the thirty-four inches of the Hyacinthine macaw. This largest and most beautiful of parrots is also, given due affection, the very gentlest of them – just as well, considering the damage it can do when it so chooses, with its enormous, powerful, all black beak. Apart from fruit and nuts, Hyacinthine macaws have been known to eat small carnivores, but whether these generally form a normal part of their diet I do not know.

NUT AND SEED EATERS:

Under this heading come most of Australia's cockatoo families, so for comparison I have chosen the beaks of the Greater Sulphur-Crested Cockatoo and the Palm Cockatoo.

Greater Sulphur-Crested Cockatoo, Kakatoe Galerita: Like a great many other cockatoos individuals of Greater Sulphur-Crested Cockatoos are noted for their longevity. As with most parrots, they are temperamental, and teasing is liable to ruin their normally sunny dispositions. However, they generally make extremely affectionate and amusing pets, attachment to their human companions often rendering them useless for breeding. Two of my dearest American cousins, Harry and Lee Bowman, have just such a delightful pet, called Topper. The main disadvantage of these cockatoos and their close relatives, as pets, is their habit of chewing things, sign of great affection though it undoubtedly is. An entertaining example of this concerning the late King George V's pet Roseate cockatoo is given in E. J. Boosey's book, and Konrad Z. Lorenz also gives amusing accounts of them.

Chiefly nut and seed eaters, cockatoos enjoy green vegetables, walnuts, almonds, etc. In fact, the unusually powerful shape of the cockatoo beaks is designed to enable them to crack open the many excessively hard-shelled nuts, like the Kanari, found on the Australian continent and the surrounding islands. Thus their squat upper mandible fully overlaps a rather narrow lower jaw.

Palm Cockatoo, Probosciger aterrimus: Inhabiting the monsoon rain forests of New Guinea, Cape York Peninsula, Australia, and the Aru Islands, this beautiful black cockatoo has the largest, most powerful beak of them all. It certainly needs this strength to get at its staple diet – Pandanus fruit seeds. The Pandanus fruit resembles a large pineapple and each of its segments contains a small elongated kernel which is what the Palm Cockatoo is after. The kernel, however, is enveloped in a very hard fibrous covering, often up to four inches thick. One naturalist, Foreshaw, records that it took him three or four blows with a sharp axe to gain access to this kernel, yet Palm Cockatoos split these fibrous nuts without the slightest difficulty.

Likewise Palm Cockatoos have no difficulty in cracking the stony Kanari nut, yet it also eats a number of smaller nuts and seeds, in which case several are taken at one time and held in the cavity of its lower mandible. These are then pushed forward by its black-tipped, red tongue, one by one, on to the chisel edge of its lower mandible where even tiny seeds are split dexterously in two. The nut/seed meat is thrown back to a basin-like cavity at the base of its tongue, and only when this is full is the food swallowed.

Like Petz's conures, Palm Cockatoos roost at some distance from their feeding areas and also take a fair amount of trouble with their nests, making a deep platform of crossed twigs at its base, keeping eggs and/or fledglings from being flooded out in monsoon rains. If angered, it has apparently been seen to 'stamp its foot', although like the Hyacinthine macaw this huge cockatoo is reputed to be the very gentlest and affectionate of pets. Its bare pink cheek will blush with emotion of any kind, and even turn blue with cold.

GRAIN AND SEED EATERS:

As with other parrots, birds in this group also eat berries and fruits. For comparison I have taken the largest and best-known of

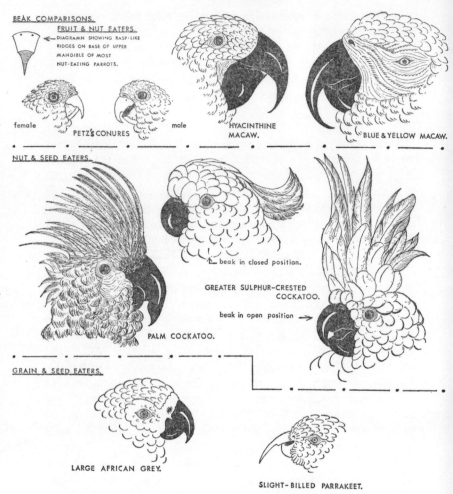

BEAK COMPARISONS.

FRUIT & NUT EATERS.

←DIAGRAMN SHOWING RASP-LIKE RIDGES ON BASE OF UPPER MANDIBLE OF MOST NUT-EATING PARROTS.

female — PETZ'S CONURES — male

HYACINTHINE MACAW.

BLUE & YELLOW MACAW.

NUT & SEED EATERS.

←beak in closed position.

GREATER SULPHUR-CRESTED COCKATOO.

beak in open position →

PALM COCKATOO.

GRAIN & SEED EATERS.

LARGE AFRICAN GREY.

SLIGHT-BILLED PARRAKEET.

the African greys *Psittacus erithacus* and Chile's Slight-Billed Parrakeet.

African Grey Parrot, Psittacus erithacus: Possibly the most renowned of birds where mimicry of the human tongue is concerned, African Greys often appear to comprehend the exact meaning of our speech, using it not only aptly, but with a great sense of comic timing. Therein perhaps lies their immense popularity as pets, for they are hardly beautiful to observe. A point in their favour as pets is that even really tame specimens

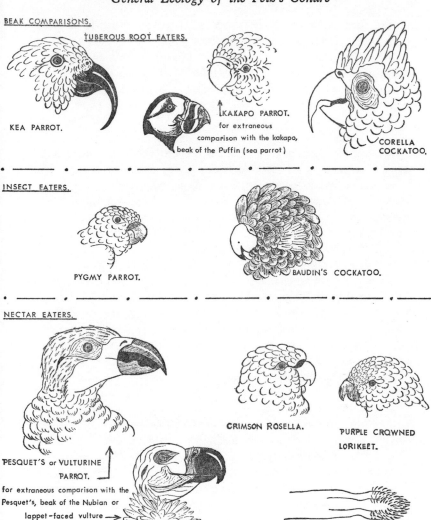

BEAK COMPARISONS.

TUBEROUS ROOT EATERS.

KEA PARROT.

↑KAKAPO PARROT.
for extraneous
comparison with the kakapo,
beak of the Puffin (sea parrot)

CORELLA
COCKATOO.

INSECT EATERS.

PYGMY PARROT.

BAUDIN'S COCKATOO.

NECTAR EATERS.

PESQUET'S or VULTURINE
PARROT.
for extraneous comparison with the
Pesquet's, beak of the Nubian or
lappet-faced vulture →

CRIMSON ROSELLA.

PURPLE CROWNED
LORIKEET.

diagramn showing brush-tongue of
most nectar eaters.

have been known to breed under good aviary conditions. E. J.
Boosey mentions in his book that these parrots were successfully
kept and bred at complete liberty by Lord Lilford. While writing
of their early history he notes that King Henry VIII, who
incidentally brought about the first law Britain ever had to protect
certain game birds, owned one. The natural staple diet of African

133

Greys, consisting of maize, seeds and ground nuts, is supplemented by berries, fruit and vegetables.

Slight-Billed Parrakeet, Enicognathus leptorhynchus: A native of Chile, little is known of the Slight-Billed Parrakeet as far as becoming a pet goes. However, being a grain-eater, it has the reputation of doing considerable damage to crops. Its basic staple foods are seeds of wheat and thistle.

TUBEROUS ROOT EATERS:

This group includes the Corella, Bloodstained, Ducorp's and Goffin's cockatoos, all from Australia or the Solomon Islands, the Kea parrot, and its near relative the Kaka, who both inhabit New Zealand, as does the comical Kakapo. For comparison I have selected the Kea, Corella and Kakapo, while for extraneous comparison with the latter, the beak of the Puffin, nicknamed the 'Sea Parrot', is included in illustration only.

Kea Parrot, Nestor notabilis: To me Keas have perhaps the most irresistibly charming characters of all the parrots I have met. Often greatly maligned for possessing an alleged but unproven capacity for killing sheep, in order to get at the fat surrounding their liver, much more likely is it that these playful and inquisitive vegetarians were occasionally seen indulging in a joy-ride on some sheep's back. But at one time farmers became so hysterical that the New Zealand Government put a price on the heads of Keas, offering 'Beak Money'. This, of course, spelled disaster and between 1920 and 1928 over 30,000 Keas were slaughtered, the disgraceful fact being that materialistically greedy townsfolk after some 'easy' money were perhaps more to blame for this than actual farmers. Happily, these brush-tongued, mountain parrots are now protected in certain island sanctuaries, but their numbers are so depleted these thoroughly delightful birds are still in danger of becoming extinct. The sagacious Duke of Bedford, who also seemed in favour of this parrot, put the lack of proof as to its carnivorous tendencies neatly in perspective by his following humorous comment: 'There is a record of a tame Kea being kept at liberty in England. She associated with the rooks but made no attempt whatever to devour the neighbouring flocks of sheep.' Ground birds, nesting in rock cavities, the Keas' long, narrow, down-curved, sharply-hooked upper mandible enables them not only to dig for tuberous root vegetables, but also to pick insects out of crannies in the rocks. (See also Chapter 7.)

Corella or Slender-Billed Cockatoo, Licmetis teniurostris: A native of Australia, the Corella's horn-coloured beak has apparently got a remarkably rapid rate of growth. E. J. Boosey records that an elderly pet of this species split its upper mandible practically from tip to base. Its owner mended the split as best he could, and so swift was the beak's growth that within three weeks the damaged portion was discarded. Doubtless this speed of growth compensates for the terrific wear and tear it must get when these cockatoos go foraging for their food, digging up tuberous root vegetables, such as yams, and bulbs of various kinds. It also eats seeds of grasses and herbs, and is particularly partial to grasshopper eggs. Speaking of the Corella's character as a pet, the Duke of Bedford referred to it as 'absurdly amiable'. It is also reputed to be a fairly good talker. The Slender-Billed Cockatoo is a comparatively rare bird, and should not be confused with the Little Corella whose flocks are quite numerous and who, incidentally, has an entirely different shaped beak.

Kakapo or Owl Parrot, Stringops habroptilus: This comical looking parrot is a native of New Zealand. Its look of cheery astonishment is possibly due to the bristle-like feathers surrounding its eyes and on its cheeks. A good climber, it is almost flightless, gliding to the ground on rather short wings. It nests amongst tree roots or in holes in the ground. As its nickname 'Owl Parrot' suggests, the Kakapo is nocturnal in its habits and fortunately has thus escaped the pet market. However, it is known to be affectionate and playful and apparently grunts with contentment when pleased with its food, which in its natural habitat consists of roots, grass weeds, vegetables, fruit, berries and seeds.

As to INSECT EATING PARROTS I am comparing the beaks of Baudin's Cockatoo and the Pygmy Parrot.

Baudin's or White-Tailed Black Cockatoo, Calyptorhynchus baudinii: Named after Baudin, a French explorer, the White-tailed Black Cockatoo, a native of Australia, is practically impossible to rear outside its own territory, as it appears that its diet consists mainly of wood-boring grubs. Moth and beetle larvae are particularly favoured by them and although insects make up the bulk of their diet, they also eat seeds of Eucalyptus, Red Gum (in hard nut), Banksias and Hakseas. Their aboriginal name 'oo-lack' adequately describes their call. Baudin's is a brown coloured parrot with a stubby crest. Its bill is greyish white with brown tips.

Pygmy Parrot, Micropsitta keiensis. A mere three inches, this tiniest of parrots is a native of New Guinea. Their diet consists partially of tree-growing fungi, but they are largely insectivorous, eating termites that they pry from the nest with their bill. Little is known about them, but they are, however, of highly nervous disposition, especially when caged, and do not therefore live long in captivity.

NECTAR EATERS:

For this last group I have selected, for beak comparison, the Purple-Crowned Lorikeet, the Vulturine or Pesquet's Parrot, and the Crimson Rosella, and as with the Kakapo, I have given (illustration only) for extraneous beak comparison with the Pesquet's that of the Nubian or lappet-faced vulture.

Vulturine or Pesquet's Parrot, Psittrichas Fulgidus: A native of New Guinea, the Vulturine parrot has, as its name suggests, a rather vulture-like shape to its elongated black beak. Its head is but scantily covered with small, bristly feathers, while the base of its bill is more or less bereft of any, which, as with vultures, may have evolved to avoid plumage becoming matted with food, for the base of its bill is often caked with the residue of fruits on whose soft pulp it feasts. Pesquet's parrots are also said to eat figs, but they mainly subsist on the nectar of large flowers. Little is known about this somewhat rare bird. Although it is said to tame well, it is by no means hardy and is therefore difficult to rear in captivity, especially outside its own climes.

Purple-Crowned Lorikeet, Glossopsitta porphyrocephala: This six-and-a-half inch native of Australia is nomadic, living mainly off flowers of various gum trees. It is easily trapped since (a) it darts towards the ground when frightened, and (b) like all other lorikeets it tends at times to become completely intoxicated on its nectar diet, and can be found completely senseless on the ground below the trees where it has been feasting. They do not, however, live long in captivity. All lorikeets are brush-tongued and probably do a good job of fertilising blossoms while sipping their nectar. Their acrobatics during feeding can be quite entertaining.

Inhabiting Victoria's Fern Gully and nicknamed 'Beautiful Lory', the *Crimson Rosella, Platycercus elegans* is perhaps the noisiest of all lorikeets. It does not attain its red and blue plumage until its third year, the young being green. Apart from nectar this lory also eats bush fruits and seeds of wattles.

To wind up the subject of beaks I thought it might be a good idea to say a few words about biting, or gripping, which is often mistaken for biting by those who are not altogether familiar with parrot ways. Since all parrots use their beaks to climb with, it is perfectly natural for them to take a good grip of a proffered finger before clambering on to one's hand, arm or shoulder. Biting as such will only occur if the would-be handler, being nervous, quickly withdraws the offered finger. This is, after all, tantamount to teasing, especially remembering that parrots only grip the finger for balance and if this is taken away they lose their sense of security, so biting is only to be expected. Generally it is only teased, frightened or fed-up birds that bite, although being sensitive creatures, they may well do so if some stranger begins getting unduly familiar, without having been properly introduced, for although in general parrots are highly sociable, they are also extremely fussy in selecting their 'nearest and dearest' human friends! Thus, before a parrot is tame, or even if tame, before it gains confidence in a new handler it is to be expected that the parrot may bite. If the handler is afraid this only makes matters worse so it is quite a good idea to wear a pair of thick leather gloves to start with. However, in early days biting is less likely to occur if titbits are offered as a matter of course before any attempt is made to get a parrot on to one's hand. One should also offer a titbit immediately prior to attempting to get the bird to perch upon one's person.

If a parrot is reluctant to release its grip after biting, do NOT flick the top of its beak, or this will only annoy the bird and lead to it biting even more savagely the next time it gets half a chance of doing so. The correct method of releasing a bite is to exert GENTLE pressure under the bird's chin with a finger of the free hand. Even more effective I personally find, is to blow a strong, quick puff of air through one's lips so as to ruffle a few feathers the wrong way. In giving itself an indignant shake to resettle them the bird will invariably release its hold on the finger. This also gives the handler a fairly adequate substitute for swearing if the pain inflicted has been particularly severe! Actually, once a parrot has complete confidence in its handler it is highly unlikely to inflict a really savage bite, though it may well nip in playful affection, and sometimes in annoyance, but even in the latter case it is quite distinct from a bite. I rather feel that even in these circumstances (unless it were ill) there would be no one more astonished than the parrot if it drew blood! However, I hope that nothing quite so drastic as this would happen to anyone acquiring a parrot; indeed I should like to wish both owner and parrot a mutual friendship as happy and rewarding as that which I have enjoyed with Solomon and Sheba.

Reference Books

In several previous chapters I referred briefly to, and quoted from, what would be an invaluable addition to the reference library of all parrot owners, if only it were more readily obtainable – in other words: *Parrots and Parrot-like Birds in Aviculture* by the Marquis of Tavistock, published by F. V. White & Co. This book is of interest to both experts and newcomers to the field. However, since only a limited number of copies were published, they are almost impossible to come by and command rare 'collectors' prices. Perhaps one day it will be revised. Meanwhile, I feel it would be well worth the effort of parrot fanciers to read through a reference library copy.

Alternatively, they may find it easier to obtain the revised American edition, published posthumously by All-Pets Books, Fond-du-lac, Wisconsin. Entitled *Parrots and Parrot-like Birds* by the (12th) Duke of Bedford, Library of Congress, card catalogue

No. 51-11580. This edition has made several changes; nonetheless our American 'cousins' have allowed the delightfully original concession, expressed in its foreword as follows: 'All the Charm of His Grace's Prose is Intact – Even the quaint English spelling has been retained'! – Who but dear 'Uncle Sam' could be quite so naively condescending?

Actually London Zoo is fortunate enough to have both copies and, thanks to the Curator, I was able to study and compare them. For instance, the Duke's section on Psittacine ailments has been replaced by an American Vet's version. One major difference occurs in the naming of several species, because American authorities often disagree with British and European experts on this matter, which inevitably leads to occasional confusion. Personally, I much prefer the American versions since, like their naming of towns and places, they are generally pleasurably apt. Anyway, since the birds are found on the American continent it seems odd that their names are not the generally accepted ones.

Albeit a case in point occurs in the naming of Solomon and Sheba's congeners. In other words, the pretty, common name for Petz's conures in both North and South America, is 'Half-Moon Parrot', a name which indeed describes them so well because of the full crescent of tiny orange feathers covering their forehead. In Great Britain and Europe, however, the name 'Half-Moon' is applied to the Golden Crowned Conure, which hardly seems so appropriate since there is no half-moon shape in the distribution of their colours. In England the Petz's is commonly known as the Orange-fronted conure, in France as Perruché à front rouge, and in Germany as Petz Keilschwanzittich. (See also Chapter 9, for Scientific name.)

Another fascinating historical book that I would recommend to parrot-lovers, having enjoyed it myself, is W. T. Greene's three-volume tome *Parrots in Captivity*, published in 1897, which is engrossing not only for its comprehensive coverage of the subject, but for its old-world phraseology, backed up by numerous helpful illustrations.

An excellent and relatively contemporary parrot book is *Parrots, Cockatoos and Macaws* by Edward J. Boosey, who, incidentally, illustrated *Parrots and Parrot-like Birds in Aviculture* by the Marquis of Tavistock. His own book, published by Barrie & Rockliff, is sparsely illustrated with competent but rather dull photographs by his partner at the Keston Bird Farm, Alec Brooksbank. In it Boosey provides an extremely interesting section on the little known history of parrots, amusing personal anecdotes, and, although it lacks the helpful veterinary advice of the Duke's book, an otherwise comprehensive coverage of his subject. As the title indicates there is no mention of conures or parrakeets. It is nonetheless a most useful handbook.

Somewhat filling the gap left by Mr Boosey's book, is one by David Seth-Smith, M.B.O.U., F.Z.S., a former curator at London Zoo, entitled *Parrakeets, Being A Practical Handbook To Those Species Kept In Captivity.* There are two editions, 1902 and 1936 published by R. H. Porter.

Index